ADVERTISING
CHARACTER COLLECTIBLES

An Identification & Value Guide

Warren Dotz

cb

COLLECTOR BOOKS
A Division of Schroeder Publishing Co., Inc.

Searching For A Publisher?

We are always looking for knowledgeable people considered to be experts within their fields. If you feel that there is a real need for a book on your collectible subject and have a large comprehensive collection, contact Collector Books.

Photography: Colin McRae
Copy Editing: Robyn Talman
Cover Design: Beth Summers
Book Design: Karen Geary

Additional copies of this book may be ordered from:

COLLECTOR BOOKS
P.O. Box 3009
Paducah, Kentucky 42002-3009

@ $17.95. Add $2.00 for postage and handling.

Copyright: Warren Dotz, 1993
Updated values, 1997

Printed by IMAGE GRAPHICS, INC., Paducah, Kentucky

DEDICATION

To the Dotz and Lee Families.

ACKNOWLEDGMENTS ————————————

I wish to acknowledge and thank the following friends, collectors, and acquaintances for their warm support over the years.

Annette and Jeff Usall

Teddy Schapiro

Andy Levison

Ed Polish

Jeff Errick

Sue and Richard Sternfeld

Jim Bauer

Nancy Boatman

Jack and Lana Obrian

Jim Ed Garrett

Ellen Weis

John Gillispie

Mike Lirones

Todd Strelow

Jim Waite

Greg Favors

Phil Arthurhultz

James Myers

Graham Trievel

Jim Rash

Nick Franovich

John Conrad

James Elkind

Joseph Saine

Roger Johnson

Dan Driskoll

Judy Posner

Stephen Veltman

Brian Razzi

Roger Brittan

James Maley

Randy Jones

Dan Goodsell

Dwayne Pike

Dennis Clark

Keith Schneider

Liz Cormier

Mike and Barbara Schwarz

Bob and Janice Johnson

Tom Demy

Mike Frigerio

Lucille Kemerling

Gary Kraut

Paul Scharfman

Liz Zerlin

Frank Gallucci

Gerry Rouff

Steve Powers

Roland Coover

Lou Criscione

Warren Pemberton

Stephanie Horvath

Keith and Judy Lyttle

John Favors

Linda and Ron Hill

Laura and Louie Grubb

CORPORATE ACKNOWLEDGMENTS

Corporate trademarks are used in the text of this publication only as part of the company story. Trademarks and brand names appear with an initial capital letter in accordance with the United States Trademark Association's special rules to protect trademarks. Therefore, we are using this corporate acknowledgment page to assure all those concerned that each of the trademark logos, brand names, and ad characters used in the text are indeed owned and registered or common trademarks of the company or agency mentioned with it, and cannot be used in any other form. In some cases, we have used an older trademark or advertising character because of its historical interest to the collector. This does not mean we are unaware of a newer version of the mark or the copyright, trademark, and registered privileges connected with the marks.

Corporate designations and product brand names appearing in the legends of this publication are used only as part of the collectible description. To the best of our knowledge, these companies owned the rights to the trademark character at the time the collectible was issued. We are aware that in some cases the registered trademark is no longer owned by the company mentioned with it, or that the company's corporate name has been modified.

To those companies that assisted on this project, we say thank you. We have tried to comply with the wishes of the companies in as much as corporate policy did not interfere with the rules of free speech. We have written to each of the companies whose histories are included in this book to verify the accuracy of the company history, as well as to indicate our intended use of each trademark.

We wish to acknowledge the following companies and advertising agencies for their assistance:

American Home Food Products, Inc.
ARCO
Anheuser-Busch, Inc.
Borden, Inc.
Brady Enterprises, Inc.
Brown Shoe Company
Brown & Williamson Tobacco Corporation
Buster Brown Apparel, Inc.
California Raisin Advisory Board
Campbell Soup Company
Chiquita Brands International, Inc.
Del Monte USA
Domino's Pizza, Inc.
Dutch Boy Paints
E. C. Publications, Inc.
Elias Brothers Restaurants, Inc.
Exxon Corporation
Facit AB
Fleishman Hillard, Inc.
Foote, Cone & Belding
General Mills, Inc.
Group 243 Incorporated
Heinz USA
Kellogg Company
Kentucky Fried Chicken
Leo Burnett USA

Mack Trucks, Inc.
McDonald's Corporation
Marriottt Corporation
Michelin Tire Corporation
Miles Inc.
Nabisco Brand, Inc.
Oscar Mayer Foods Corporation
Pabst Brewing Company
Piel Bros. Ltd.
The Pillsbury Company
Planters Division of Nabisco, Inc.
The Procter & Gamble Company
The Quaker Oats Company
Radio Corporation of America
Reddy Communications, Inc.
The Seven-Up Company
Sinclair Oil Corporation
StarKist Seafood Company
Sun-Maid Growers of California
Sunshine Biscuits, Inc.
Travelodge (Forte Hotels, Inc.)
The Uhlmann Company
United States Department of Agriculture, Forest Service
United States Postal Service
Jay Ward Productions, Inc.
Western Exterminator Company

TABLE OF CONTENTS

FOREWORD

Advertising character collectibles come in many different forms – so many in fact that I have decided to limit the scope of this book to figural advertising. I define figural advertising as a three-dimensional representation of the character itself, including store displays, statuettes, squeeze toys, banks, radios, inflatables, and dolls. I have excluded those three-dimensional objects that are not truly in the shape of a character, such as store signs. I have also decided not to include any plush, cloth, or clothed promotional, advertising dolls. Although important to the field of advertising character collectibles, these items have been studied in other books.

For the purposes of this book, an advertising character's primary function is to promote a company, brand name, or product. In some cases, the character is the company's registered logo or trademark. In other cases, he or she can be the registered brand mark for one or more of a company's products.

Some ad characters were used for many years and are still in use. Others were used only once for a particular promotion. It is always interesting to see how characters were modernized over the years, and how two-dimensional logos were translated to the figural form.

As with any ground rules, there are some gray areas as to who or what qualifies as an advertising character. Buster Brown, for example, had originally appeared in a long-running newspaper cartoon before he was eventually licensed to over a hundred companies for their promotional use. Most people, however, remember Buster and Tige from buying shoes as kids in the Buster Brown Shoe Store. Since Buster has put in more service as an ad character than a cartoon character, I have included him in this book. On the other hand, I have excluded characters such as the Flintstones and the Pink Panther, since they are truly cartoon characters, licensed to promote various brand names.

I hope you enjoy this edition of *Advertising Character Collectibles*. If you have any items for sale or information that might merit presentation in future editions, feel free to contact me. Inquiries and comments may be directed by correspondence to:

Warren Dotz
2999 Regent Street, Suite 300
Berkeley, California 94705

READING THE LEGENDS

NAME OF ADVERTISING CHARACTER
Corporation associated with character
Product, brand name, enterprise or service
Composition and function of collectible
Specific year or estimated decade of issuance
Height in inches
Current value

Example:
Charlie the Tuna
StarKist Foods, Inc., Canned tuna
Plastic telephone, c. 1980s, 10". $50.00.

In most cases, the registered trademark character name is used. In those instances where a registered name did not exist or was not known, we supplied a generally accepted name or one that would be descriptive and useful.

CORPORATION ASSOCIATED WITH CHARACTER
The corporate designation legend corresponds to the company which owned the rights to the trademark character at the time the collectible was issued. In those instances where this information was not available we supplied the name of the corporation that currently owns the trademark rights to the character. It should also be noted that although these corporations authorized the use of their licensed advertising characters, most collectibles were manufactured by outside firms specializing in store display, toys, and vinyl, plastic and ceramic molding (e.g., Riverdale Plastics, F & F Mold and Dye Works).

In most cases, figural advertising items were issued as company authorized promotional premiums and point-of-purchase store displays. Some were issued as product containers or in-house employee gifts and awards. Occasionally, a collectible was released as a licensed or unlicensed direct-to-the-public toy or novelty gift.

Chapter 1

RESTAURANTS AND FAST FOODS

Big Boy Elias Brothers Restaurants, Inc.

In 1936, Bob Wian took his life savings, a significant part of which came from the sale of his car, and his dad's $50 loan, and bought a ten-seat diner on the main drag in Glendale, California. He named it Bob's Pantry. Within the year, Bob had perfected the first double-deck cheeseburger and called it the "Big Boy." The burger became so popular that the diner was rechristened "Bob's Big Boy," using as its symbol a caricature of one of Wian's chubby young customers.

As the popularity of the Big Boy increased, the restaurants began to pop up around Southern California. From there, they spread to other parts of the country as franchises, under the names of Elias, JB's, Frisch's, and Shoney's. In 1967, the Marriott Corporation acquired Big Boy, which by that time had become a national chain.

For many years the boyish Big Boy served the company well as an ideal, nostalgic burger-bearing mascot. The character was even slimmed down from down-right fat to merely rotund as the chain's menu became more health conscious. By 1984, Marriott wanted to tell the public about its restaurants' renovated, contemporary decor and expanded menus and salad bars. The corporation wondered whether Big Boy's ties to the past might be hindering sales growth. Did the public's image of the checkered-pants Bob say "light, airy, and green?"

With the help of its ad agency, Big Boy Restaurants launched a magnificently successful, in-store and TV campaign – "Should he stay or should he go?" After spirited campaigning and media debating, diners were asked to vote on the issue of the Big Boy's fate. In fact, one memorable commercial, directed by the comedian David Steinberg, teamed Speedy Alka-Seltzer, the Michelin Man, and the Dutch Boy as the "Committee to Save the Big Boy." With the battle cry *"Are we gonna let 'em retire our buddy?"* the team hit the street, canvassing a neighborhood door to door. Speedy ended the commercial stating beseechingly, *"His fate is in your hands."*

Would the Big Boy be sent to hamburger heaven? When all the votes were counted, the Big Boy won in a landslide. The company notes that they would have retired the character had he lost.

Big Boy
Marriott Corporation, Big Boy restaurant chain. Papier maché bank, c. 1970s, 8".
$450.00.

Big Boy
Marriott Corporation, Big Boy restaurant chain. Papier maché bobbin' head, c. 1960s, 8". $900.00.

Big Boy
Marriott Corporation, Big Boy restaurant chain. Vinyl electrical nite-lite, c. 1970s, 7". $65.00 each.

Big Boy
Frisch's Restaurants, Inc., Frisch's Big Boy restaurant chain. PVC statuette, c. 1984, 2½". $50.00.

Big Boy
Marriott Corporation, Big Boy restaurant chain. Molded vinyl banks, c. 1970s –present, 9". $25.00 each.

Big Boy
Marriott Corporation, Big Boy Restaurants of America. Molded vinyl banks, c. 1970s–present, 9". Left – $10.00; right – $30.00.

Big Boy
Marriott Corporation, Big Boy restaurant chain. Ceramic salt and pepper shakers, c. 1950s, 4½". $250.00 set.

Colonel Sanders   Kentucky Fried Chicken

Harland Sanders first started cooking chicken in a kitchen behind a gas station in Corbin, Kentucky, a small town near the edge of the Appalachian Mountains. He was also the station operator and cashier. Business grew steadily as his reputation for good food attracted tourists who made it a point to stop by. Word spread about his finger-licking good chicken, and in 1935 the governor made him an official Kentucky Colonel in recognition of his contribution to the state's cuisine. His recipe was enhanced further when the Colonel discovered he could use the newly developed pressure cooker to fry chicken in a faster and less greasy manner – a use its inventor had never dreamed. By the end of World War II, the thriving Sanders Court and Cafe included a motel and expansive restaurant.

Things were going well for the Colonel until 1956 when the Federal government built a new interstate highway that bypassed Corbin, putting him out of business. At 66, the Colonel decided to franchise his most valuable asset – the regionally famous blend of eleven herbs and spices. He began to call on other restaurant owners, teaching them how to cook his Kentucky Fried Chicken. Included in the bargain was his secret blend of herbs and spices, which he kept in a jar in his car. Each restaurant was charged 4¢ for every chicken cooked the Colonel's way.

To publicize his new franchise business, Sanders began dressing in a white suit and black string tie. With his own white goatee, he looked like a traditional Kentucky Colonel and soon became the walking, talking trademark of his business. When the Colonel sold his franchises in 1964, the Kentucky Fried Chicken operation was 600 restaurants strong. He had become so popular by then that the new owners asked him to stay on as the company's greatest promotional asset.

The Colonel's new role also launched his television career. He appeared on talk shows and programs such as *What's My Line*. He was most popular with children, who viewed him as sort of a grandfather/

Santa Claus figure. The Colonel died in 1980 at the age of 90.

His blend of herbs and spices has remained a well-kept secret. Only a handful of people know it, and they have signed strict confidentiality contracts. In the 1960s, the Colonel appeared in a rather bizarre commercial. A group of angry housewives kidnapped and tied him up, but he still would not reveal his secret blend!

Col. Sanders
Kentucky Fried Chicken, restaurant chain. Plastic bank, c. 1960s, 12½". $25.00.

Col. Sanders
Kentucky Fried Chicken, restaurant chain. Plastic salt and pepper shakers, c. 1960s, 3½". $55.00.

Col. Sanders
Kentucky Fried Chicken, restaurant chain. Plastic bank, c. 1970s, 8". $35.00.

Col. Sanders
Kentucky Fried Chicken, restaurant chain. Plastic bobbin' head, c. 1960s, 7". $75.00.

Col. Sanders and Mrs. Sanders
Kentucky Fried Chicken, restaurant chain. Plastic salt and pepper shakers, bust figures of Col. and Mrs. Sanders, 4". Plastic bank, Col. Sanders with restaurant, 6". Plastic finger puppet of Col. Sanders, 1". Shakers, set – $125.00; Bank – $45.00; Finger puppet – $12.00.

Noid® Domino's Pizza, Inc.

© 1992 Domino's Pizza, Inc.

Noid ®
Domino's Pizza, Inc., restaurant chain. PVC bendable figure, c. 1980s, 5". $5.00.

In the summer of 1985, Domino's ad agency, Group 243, set out to create a memorable character that would personify the average person's fears about delivered pizza. The company hoped to increase public awareness of Domino's Pizza, and at the same time, humorously communicate all the things it does to deliver a hot, fresh pie. The result was the devilish Noid (short for Dominoid), a character who was the delivered pizza's worst enemy. If your pizza arrives cold – the Noid did it; stuck to the box – the Noid did it. By *"avoiding the Noid,"* Domino's always achieved its goal.

Although the Noid enjoyed a spiritual kinship with such other stubborn losers as Charlie the Tuna and the Trix Rabbit, he attained the singular distinction of being the first advertising mascot hell-bent on wrecking the very product he promotes. With his arsenal of pizza crushers and box-busting jackhammers, ads featuring Will Vinton Productions' Claymation Noid brought Domino's merchandising success and national consumer awareness.

Noid ®
Domino's Pizza, Inc., restaurant chain. PVC figures, c. 1980s, 2½". $2.00 each.

Ronald McDonald   McDonald's Corporation

Dick and Mac MacDonald operated a barbecue stand with carhops in San Bernardino, California from 1940 to 1948. In 1948, they reopened as a self-service hamburger restaurant. McDonald's Drive-in's exceptionally fast service, low prices, and no-tipping policy had attracted a growing number of customers. In 1954, Ray Kroc, a 52-year old milkshake mixer distributor, visited the two brothers. Kroc wanted to find out why a restaurant as small as theirs needed eight of his machines. He was amazed to discover their volume of business. When the McDonalds, who by that time had a number of franchises, told him that they didn't want any more stores, Kroc arranged to become their exclusive franchise agent. He eventually bought them out in 1961, and the rest is fast food history.

The first McDonald's mascot was the bun-headed Speedee, who embodied the chain's main attributes. He had a wink in his eye, and carried a sign announcing "I'm Speedee" or "15¢" – the price of a McDonald's hamburger. Speedee reigned atop the distinctive golden arches of McDonald's stores until 1962, when the arches replaced him as the company logo. McDonald's successful jingle, *"Look for the golden arches,"* made them the more recognizable trademark.

It was not until 1963 that Ronald McDonald made his first appearance for franchises in Washington, DC. One of the first Ronald McDonalds was the now-famous weatherman, Willard Scott. In 1966, Ronald appeared nationally for the first time in the Macy's Thanksgiving Day Parade. He was named the company's official spokesman.

Throughout the 1970s and 1980s, Ronald's popularity continued to grow, as he appeared on national "McDonaldland" television commercials and personally opened 9,000 McDonald's stores. The company claims that Ronald McDonald is recognized by 96% of American children. He is also an international star. Since the "R" sound is not part of the Japanese language, he is known in Japan as "Donald McDonald." In Hong Kong, where family relationships are particularly important, he is called "McDonald Suk Suk" ("Uncle McDonald").

Ronald McDonald
McDonald's Corporation, restaurant chain.
Plastic telephone, 1985, 10". $125.00.

Ronald McDonald
McDonald's Corporation, restaurant chain. Plastic bank,
c. 1980s, 7½". $30.00.

Ronald McDonald
McDonald's Corporation, restaurant chain. PVC and glow-
in-the-dark plastic, c. 1980s, 3". $10.00.

Miscellaneous Companies

Acey
Arctic Circle Drive-In, restaurant chain. Painted plaster bank, c. 1960s, 7". $45.00.

Chuck E. Cheese
Pizza Time Theater, Inc., restaurant and entertainment chain. Plastic bank, c. 1980s, 5½". $10.00.

Chicken Delight
Chicken Delight International, Inc., take-out restaurant chain. Molded vinyl bank, c. 1960s, 6". $115.00.

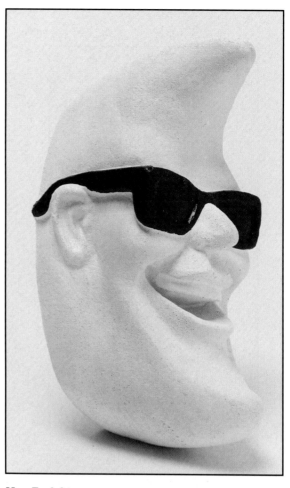

Hobo Joe
Colony Kitchens, Inc. Hobo Joe's Restaurants. Molded vinyl bank, c. 1980s, 12". $35.00.

Mac Tonight
McDonald's Corporation, restaurant chain. Foam finger puppet, 1988, 6". $20.00.

Mac Tonight
McDonald's Corporation, restaurant chain. PVC figurines, c. 1980s, 3½". $3.00 each.

Mac Tonight
McDonald's Corporation, restaurant chain. PVC figurines, c. 1980s, 2½". $3.00 each.

Menehunes
Trader Vics, restaurant chain. Molded vinyl swizzle stick ornaments, c. 1970s, 2½". $25.00 pair.

Pappy Parker
Marriott Corporation, Pappy Parkers Chicken House restaurants. Molded vinyl dolls, 1973, 6½". $40.00 each.

Pizza Hut Pete
Pizza Hut, Inc., restaurant chain. Plastic bank, 1969, 7½". $30.00.

Pizza Inn Man
Pizza Inn Incorporated, restaurant chain. Plastic telephone, c. 1980s, 10". $70.00.

Scott's Chicken
Scott's Fried Chicken, restaurant chain. Plastic banks, c. 1970s, 10". $60.00 each.

Sonny
Sonny's "Dilly Burgers," restaurant chain. Plaster ashtray, c. 1950s, 9". $750.00.

Shakey Chef
Shakey's Pizza Parlors, restaurant chain. Ceramic bank, c. 1970s, 6". $35.00.

Smokquee
The Royal (Boise, ID), hotel and restaurant. Ceramic salt and pepper shakers, c. 1950s, 4". $175.00.

Sylvester C. Host and friends
Sea Host, Inc., seafood restaurants. Plastic push puppets, 1969, 4½". $45.00 each.

Tee and Eff
Tastee-Freez International, ice cream and restaurant chain. Ceramic salt and pepper shakers, c. 1960s, 4". $55.00.

The Little Fisherman
No. 9 Fisherman's Grotto (Fisherman's Wharf, San Fransico, CA), restaurant. Painted metal statuette, c. 1940s, 3". $30.00.

The Pancake Man
International House of Pancakes, restaurant chain. Rubber figurines, c. 1960s, 2½". $20.00 each.

Wendy
Wendy's International, restaurant chain. Plastic statuette, c. 1980s, 2". $10.00.

Chapter 2

BREAKFAST CEREALS

Cap'n Crunch   The Quaker Oats Company

In the early 1960s, The Quaker Oats Company took note that it had no pre-sweetened, ready-to-eat cereal to appeal to the 40 million hungry mouths of the under-ten age group. Since market research had determined that kids preferred crunchy snacks, the company began developing a cereal with this characteristic. At the same time, the advertising department developed a trademark character strong in juvenile appeal – a salty, bumbling, comic sea-captain named Cap'n Crunch.

As the first experimental batches of Cap'n Crunch cereal were emerging from plant extruders in 1963, the S.S. Guppy sailed out of Jay Ward's animation studio in Hollywood. This began a series of adventures for old Cap'n Crunch, his canine first-mate, Seadog, and a crew of four children. In his first appearance, the Cap'n, with his blue Napoleonic hat and white moustache, assured his viewers that the cereal "has to be good because they named it after me."

In most of the commercials, everyone is crazy for the cereal – especially Jean Lafoote, the scheming but inept pirate who always conspires to steal the Guppy's crunchy cargo. Jay Ward Productions, known for its immortal characters, Rocky and Bullwinkle, Boris and Natasha, and Mr. Peabody and Sherman, gave the commercials irreverent wit and style.

Cap'n Crunch fan clubs began springing up all over the country. The cereal quickly went international – *Capitaine Crouche* in French-speaking areas of Canada and *Kaptajn Kras* in Scandinavia. Within a year, Cap'n Crunch cereal was outselling 55 competitors.

Cap'n Crunch
The Quaker Oats Company, Cap'n Crunch cereal. Plastic premium, c. 1980s. $3.00.

Jean LaFoote and Cap'n Crunch
The Quaker Oats Company, Cap'n Crunch cereal. Molded vinyl banks, 1975, 8". Left – $80.00; right – $45.00.

Marky Maypo   American Home Food Products, Inc. The Uhlmann Company

In 1956, Heublein, Inc. was concerned about the sagging sales of its maple-flavored oat cereal, Maypo. Before giving up on the product, the company decided to try one last TV spot. That commercial introduced Marky, a cartoon boy who fancied himself a rough-and-ready cowboy – one who refused, at first, to eat the sponsor's product. In an effort to coax the reluctant boy, his Uncle Ralphie tried the cereal himself. After swallowing a spoonful, Uncle Ralphie beamed with delight, prompting the envious Marky to scream, *"I want my Maypo!"* Marky then proceeded to gulp it all down.

Marky and his oddball family delighted viewers for years, and Maypo is still thriving to this day.

Marky Maypo
American Home Food Products, Inc., Maypo Oat Cereal. Molded vinyl bank, c. 1960s, 9". $50.00.

The Quaker Oats Man   The Quaker Oats Company

The Quaker Oats man first appeared on boxes of steel-cut oats made by a small mill in Ravenna, Ohio. Possibly with an eye on the larger Quaker-population nearby, or the fact that one of the owners was of Quaker descent, the Quaker Oats man turned out to be an ideal symbol. Dressed in typical clothing and carrying a scroll inscribed with the word "Pure," he carried all the virtuous implications of the Quaker religion and instilled buyer confidence. When the Quaker Mill Company registered this "figure of a man in Quaker garb" in 1877, he became America's first registered-trademark for a breakfast cereal.

None of the partners in the Quaker Mill was an experienced businessman, however, and the venture languished. It even passed through the hands of a distiller, who extended the Quaker symbol to a whiskey he bottled. The mill was at last sold to the dynamic and innovative Henry Crowell. He came up with many "firsts," among them the use of four-color, printed cartons which displayed the Quaker trademark and offered recipes and product information. Consumers who would cut out the Quaker figure and mail it to the company were offered attractive premiums, further impressing the trademark image upon them. Crowell was also the first to produce a miniature of his carton for house-to-house samplings. He even filled entire trains with Quaker Oats, giving out free samples on stops along the way.

By 1893, the Quaker symbol was changed to reflect the company's goodwill, and the gaunt and austere Quaker gave way to a genial, fat-bellied one. Through a succession of mergers and takeovers, the Quaker brand became the principal product of the American Cereal Company, which is now The Quaker Oats Company.

Quaker
The Quaker Oats Company, Quaker Oats cereal and products. Plastic mug, c. 1950s, 4". $15.00.

Quaker
The Quaker Oats Company, Quaker Oats cereal and products. Plastic sugar shaker, c. 1970s, 5½". $70.00.

Snap! Crackle! and Pop!® Kellogg Company

® Kellogg Company
© 1992 Kellogg Company

In 1928, Kellogg Company introduced *Rice Krispies*® cereal. The company's advertising agency at that time was quick to capitalize on the most distinctive feature of the toasted rice cereal – the noise it makes in milk. To communicate this new cereal's unique trait, they chose the slogan *Snap! Crackle! and Pop!*®.

The *Snap! Crackle!* and *Pop!*® names first appeared on boxes of *Kellogg's*® *Rice Krispies*® in 1932. Within a year, a tiny gnome, wearing a baker's cap and carrying a spoon, showed up on a side panel. Although unnamed and appearing solo, this character was the prototype for *Snap!*®. By the end of the decade, he was joined by his pals, *Crackle!*® and *Pop!*®.

The *Snap! Crackle!* and *Pop!*® characters originally appeared as gnomes with huge hats, ears and noses. The trio has evolved over the years, adopting more human-like features. Their hats, however, have changed very little. *Snap!*® still wears a baker's hat; *Crackle!*®, a red or striped stocking cap; *Pop!*® a British military hat.

Snap! Crackle! and *Pop!*® are still at work on *Kellogg's*® *Rice Krispies*® boxes and advertisments. They have appeared in hundreds of ads and commercials and are often found singing and dancing and revealing three distinct personalities. Their most popular jingle, *"Snap!, Crackle!, Pop! Rice Krispies"* has been used by Kellogg Company for over 24 years.

Snap! Crackle! and *Pop!*® also own the double distinction of being both the first and longest advertising characters to represent Kellogg Company products. The characters are international stars as well. For example, in Sweden, they're *Piff! Paff!* and *Puff!*®, and Germany, *Knisper! Knasper!* and *Knusper!*®

Snap! Crackle! Pop!®
Kellogg Company, *Rice Krispies*® cereal. Plastic push puppets, 1984, 4". $20.00 each.

Snap! Crackle! Pop! ®
Kellogg Company, *Rice Krispies* ® cereal. Molded vinyl squeeze toys, 1975, 7½". Top – $30.00 each;
Bottom – $35.00 each.

Tony The Tiger® Kellogg Company

TM, ® Kellogg Company
© 1992 Kellogg Company

Tony The Tiger™ made his debut in 1952 as part of a series of animal illustrations appearing on boxes of *Sugar Frosted Flakes*® cereal. *Tony*® proved to be much more popular than *Katie the Kangaroo, Newt the Gnu,* and *Zeke the Zebra.* With the slogan,

"I'm here to loudly state, Sugar Frosted Flakes are Gr-r-reat!," he quickly was promoted as the product's official spokesman.

In his early days, *Tony*® looked different. He was thinner and walked on all fours with a head shaped like a football. Over the years, *Tony*® has appeared in many *Kellogg's Frosted Flakes*® commercials, including various live-action and slap-stick situations. In his early appearances, *Tony*® was featured with his son, *Tony Jr.*®, who became the trademark character for *Kellogg's Frosted Rice* cereal. By the 1970s, *Tony*® had an entire family, including a doting mother, wife, and a daughter, *Antoinette.*

Although *Kellogg's Frosted Flakes*® cereal remains his first love, Kellogg Company advanced *Tony's*® career from product spokesman to full-fledged goodwill ambassador for the entire company. His image has appeared on numerous promotions and premiums, a hot-air balloon, and a statue in the courtyard of the Battle Creek, Michigan, production facility.

Tony The Tiger™
Kellogg Company, *Sugar Frosted Flakes*® cereal.
Plastic transistor AM radio, 1980, 7". $30.00.

Tony The Tiger™
Kellogg Company, *Sugar Frosted Flakes*® cereal.
Vinyl squeeze toy, 1974, 7½". $40.00.

Trix Rabbit General Mills, Inc.

Although Trix cereal was introduced in 1954, the Trix Rabbit did not become the product's spokesman until 1959. In those early years, Trix was among the first pre-sweetened cereals on the market. With its red, yellow, and orange colors, Trix quickly became a favorite with children. And with its motto, *"Trix are for kids,"* the Rabbit was born.

The floppy-eared, conniving Rabbit hated carrots, but loved Trix. He used various disguises to obtain a bowlful of the cereal – only to be exposed, in his excitement, as a Rabbit, not a kid.

For years, General Mills received letters from children, pleading to let the poor Rabbit have some Trix. Finally, in 1976, the company decided to give the Rabbit his big chance. During the U.S. presidential elections, a campaign was held in Trix commercials. By mailing in box top ballots, young viewers could cast their vote as to whether the Rabbit should be allowed a taste of his beloved Trix.

Support was overwhelming. The Rabbit was finally given one bowl of Trix, and went berserk with ecstasy. But the continuing theme remains, "Silly Rabbit, Trix are for kids."

Trix Rabbit
General Mills, Inc., Trix cereal. Molded vinyl squeeze toy, 1977, 9". $35.00.

Miscellaneous Cereals

Apple Jacks®
Kellogg Company, *Apple Jacks*® cereal. Plastic mug with hat lid, c. 1970s, 3½". $40.00.

Quisp
The Quaker Oats Company, Quisp cereal. Papier maché bank, c. 1960s, 6½". $900.00.

Toucan Sam®
Kellogg Company, *Fruit Loops*® cereal. Plastic push puppet and plastic figurine, 1984, 4". $20.00 each.

Twinkles
General Mills, Inc., Twinkles cereal. Plastic bank, c. 1960s, 7½". $525.00.

Chapter 3
FRUITS AND VEGETABLES

Aristocrat Tomato   H. J. Heinz Company

Trademark is used with permission of the H.J. Heinz Company.

The Heinz Aristocrat Tomato man was first used in the mid-1930s to publicize Heinz Tomato Juice. The company wanted to make the point that its juice was the "aristocrat" of all tomato juices. To create a memorable advertising campaign, this seed of an idea was developed into the Aristocrat Tomato.

In his first ad, the Aristocrat Tomato appeared with portraits of his father and grandfather, each "tomato-head" sporting the top hat and ascot of his day. For decades, Heinz peppered his image on its ads for ketchup, soup, and juice. This tomato man was originally designed only to wear the formal clothes of the aristocratic world – tuxedo, cut-away vest, and silk hat. In later years, however, the Aristocrat Tomato was also dressed in the garb of a farmer and an engineer.

Aristocrat Tomato (top)
H. J. Heinz Company, tomato juice, ketchup, and food products. Composition statuette, 1939, 6". $250.00.

Aristocrat Tomato (bottom)
H. J. Heinz Company, tomato juice, ketchup, and food products. Composition ornament, 1939, 2½". $100.00.

Aristocrat Tomato
H. J. Heinz Company, tomato juice, ketchup, and food products. Plastic talking alarm clock, c. 1980s, 9½". $175.00.

The California Raisins California Raisin Advisory Board

The story of the California Raisin begins in the fertile Central Valley of California, the self-proclaimed raisin capital of the world. In the 1940s, the raisin business was haunted by oversupply and shrinking profits. To promote the use and sales of raisins, the individual growers formed the California Raisin Advisory Board (CALRAB). For years, the Board concocted raisin recipes, planned raisin fairs, and sponsored an annual Raisin Queen beauty contest. In the 1970s, CALRAB tried to promote the raisin as a healthful adult snack, achieving only moderate success. CALRAB's goal for the 1980s was to change the public's somewhat blasé attitude toward the raisin.

Not even CALRAB could have anticipated that a conga line of Claymation raisin characters, singing an old Marvin Gaye tune, would put such a wrinkle in the dried fruit business. But that's just what Foote, Cone & Belding's and Will Vinton Productions' "The California Raisins" did in 1986 to the Motown sound of *I Heard It Through the Grapevine*.

Television viewers were amazed and amused to see the soulful, singing raisins strut their stuff, while turning up their noses at less nutritious snacks. One spot had the four clay crooners add some life to a construction worker's lunch pail, by transforming a boring sandwich into a night club stage. A blockbuster musical record album soon followed and the California Raisins were an international hit. Raisin sales jumped 20%. Subsequently, the original four raisins have been joined by a host of supporting stars, including Ray Charles and a Michael Jackson Raisin, whose rock concert performance came complete with his distinctive silver glove.

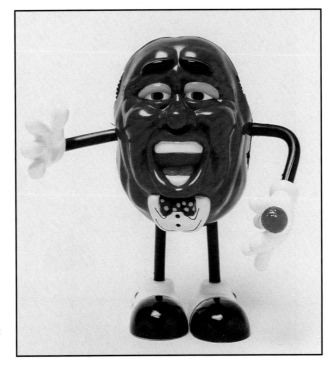

California Raisin
California Raisin Advisory Board, California raisins. Plastic and PVC AM-FM transistor radio, 1988, 7½". $50.00.

California Raisin
California Raisin Advisory Board, California raisins. PVC figurine, c. 1980s, 2½". $2.00.

"Michael" California Raisin
California Raisin Advisory Board, California raisins. PVC figurine, c. 1980s, 4". $10.00.

The California Raisins
Del Monte Corporation/CALRAB, Del Monte fruit snacks. PVC figures and plastic sandwich stage with musical chip that plays *I Heard It Through The Grapevine*, 1987, 1" and 2½". $35.00.

Chiquita Banana   Chiquita Brands International, Inc.

In 1944, the United Fruit Company envisioned its armada of ships, which was aiding the war effort, soon to be back in the Caribbean banana trade. To raise the public's banana consciousness, it embarked on what it thought would be an educational campaign to promote two basic banana facts – bananas taste better if eaten when their peels have brown spots and bananas should be allowed to ripen at room temperature.

With a catchy Calypso beat and a tune by Garth Montgomery and Len MacKenzie, United Fruit introduced its brain child – the singing, dancing Chiquita Banana.

> *I'm Chiquita Banana and I've come to say,*
> *Bananas have to ripen in a certain way....*
> *Bananas like the climate of the very, very tropical*
>   *equator,*
> *So you should never put banana in the refrigerator.*

By the end of the war, Chiquita's appealing song was a big disc jockey, dance band, and jukebox hit. In addition to her commercial airings, paid for by United Fruit, the song was performed by Carmen Miranda, Xavier Cugat, and many others. Chiquita eventually became a star of stage and screen as well. Her blue and yellow labels still grace each and every bunch of United Fruit bananas, now called Chiquita Brands International, Inc.

Chiquita Banana
United Fruit Company, bananas. Sebastian miniature, 1951, 4". $550.00.

The Jolly Green Giant   The Pillsbury Company

In the early 1920s, the Minnesota Valley Canning Company discovered a new variety of pea in Europe. The new pea was much larger than the small, smooth and round peas that the majority of Americans preferred. Most big peas were old and tough, but these new, giant green peas were so flavorful and tender that the company decided not to apologize, but to brag about their size.

When the company applied for a trademark for the new pea, its attorney in Washington, DC said that the words "green giant" were descriptive, and therefore might not be patentable. He suggested putting a giant on the label as a symbol. By claiming that "green giant" referred to the giant rather than the pea, perhaps a patent could be obtained.

The first "Green Giant" appeared in 1925. Borrowed from a book of Grimm's Fairy Tales, he wore a scowl and a scruffy bearskin. He looked more Neanderthal than giant-like. And, he wasn't even green – he was white!

Two years later, the company logically made the giant green, but it was not until 1935 that a young Chicago ad man, Leo Burnett, gave the giant his appealing demeanor. His Paul Bunyanesque giant stood straight up, wore a leafy suit, smiled, and lived in the Valley of the Jolly, Ho! Ho! Ho!, Green Giant. Throughout the next decades, the Giant continued to be updated, and his popularity led to the company changing its name to Green Giant Company.

By the 1950s, the Giant was ready to embark on the road to television stardom. However, television was not an easy transition. In both animation and live forms, the closer he got to the camera, the less jolly he seemed. In fact, he looked monsterish! Finally a solution was found. Instead of creating a giant-sized Giant, a miniature valley was built in which the Giant could stand off in the distance, legendary and romantic.

With the growing variety of Green Giant products, the Giant continued to be modified. For example, when frozen foods were added, he donned a dashing red scarf. In 1972, he became the Green Giant that appears on labels today – the hearty, robust, outdoor type. And he finally got a pair of shoes!

Little Green Sprout   The Pillsbury Company

Up in the Valley of the Jolly Green Giant,
Lives a guy they call the Little Green Sprout.
He's not very big – about the size of a twig,
But, that's how Jolly Green Giants start out.

In 1968, Green Giant Company asked its ad agency, Leo Burnett, to develop a back-up campaign to succeed the phenomenally successful Valley of the Green Giant commercials. Many approaches were explored, with an eye toward making the new commercials not only more visually exciting than the originals, but more versatile as well. The solution came in the form of the Little Green Sprout – a child-like, sort of Huck Finn of a vegetable, always in awe of the Giant and his skills. The outgoing and talkative Sprout proved to be the perfect complement to the Giant, whose vocabulary had always been limited to three words – all of which were *"Ho"*! Fortunately, the company chose not to promote an original, but limiting, characteristic of the Sprout – if he stayed in one place too long he grew roots.

The Jolly Green Giant and Sprout
Green Giant Company, Green Giant products. Molded vinyl squeeze toys, 1975. 9½" – $75.00; 6½" – $10.00.

Little Green Sprout
Green Giant Company, Green Giant products. Plastic transistor radio, c. 1980s, 8½". $30.00. Flashlight, c. 1980s, 8½". $20.00.

The Sun Maid   Sun-Maid Growers of California

In 1912, a group of San Joaquin Valley raisin-growers formed a cooperative called the California Associated Raisin Company to promote and advertise their product. Three years later, the young co-op adopted the brand name, Sun-Maid, in reference to the fact that their raisins were "made" in the California sunshine.

The brand's play on words also suggested a personality – a pretty maid gathering the harvest and helping to prepare the raisins. At about that time, 18-year old Lorraine Collett was working at a raisin-packing farm near her home in Fresno. She and two other young women were chosen by the association to hand out boxes of raisins at the Panama-Pacific Exposition in San Francisco. Partway through the fair, she was selected to pose for the artist, Fanny Scafford, and the now world-famous, bonneted Sun-Maid trademark was born.

California Raisin and Sun Maid
Sun-Maid Growers of California/CALRAB, Sun-Maid Raisins. Molded vinyl bank, c. 1980s, 7". $17.50.

Other Products

Easy
Stokely Van Camp, canned vegetables and foods. Ceramic statuette, c. 1950s, 7½". $450.00.

Farmer Jack
Borman's, Inc., Farmer Jack supermarkets. Molded vinyl bank, 1986, 7". $35.00.

Florida Orange Bird
Florida Department of Citrus, oranges and orange juice. Plastic bank, c. 1970s, 5". $20.00. Plastic bobbin' head, c. 1970s, 7". $55.00.

Vegetable Man
Kraft, Inc., Kraft salad dressings. Molded vinyl bank, c. 1970s, 8". $300.00.

Chapter 4

FOOD PRODUCTS

The Campbell Kids Campbell Soup Company

the Kids have undergone facelifts – their eyes, noses, chins, and heights have been changed subtly to mirror contemporary appearances. Keeping with weight-conscious times, they have been slimmed down as well. However, two things have not been changed – the Kids have never had first names and their ears and necks have never shown!

In 1887, Dr. J. T. Dorrance, a young chemist, developed a line of condensed soups for Joseph Campbell's small soup company. The tasty canned soup proved quite popular. A Campbell's executive liked the school colors of Cornell University, and using those colors designed the distinctive red-and-white label that is adorned with a golden medal, an award from the 1900 Paris Exposition.

With the success of the soups, the company began advertising catchy jingles on New York City street car placards. As luck would have it, a young illustrator named Grace Wiederseim Drayton was married to one of the employees at the firm where the placards were printed. This gave her the opportunity to propose that the Campell Soup Company use some of her sketches of rosy-cheeked, cherub-like kids. Since childhood, Grace had doodled these "roly poly's," as she called them, modeling them after her own round face and upturned nose. The Campbell Soup Company considered these chubby, robust "Campbell Kids" ideal symbols for its wholesome, nourishing soups.

In the early years, Grace's kids were simply boys and girls. In later advertisements, she portrayed them as chefs, sailors, and soldiers, to name a few. Over the years, the company has issued a host of Campbell Kids premiums and dolls. During this time,

Campbell Kid Chef
Campbell Soup Company, Campbell's soups. Molded rubber squeeze toy, c. 1950s, 7". $70.00.

Campbell Kids
Campbell Soup Company, Campbell's soups. Plastic salt and pepper shakers, c. 1950s, 4½". $45.00.

Charlie The Tuna   StarKist Seafood Company

Charlie the Tuna made his big splash in advertising in 1961. In that year, StarKist decided to replace its "Fisherman" corporate logo with Charlie on its cans of tuna fish.

Charlie is a street-smart, beatnik-fish, sporting a beret and shades. In his original conception, Charlie's illustrators gave him teeth and a shark-like dorsal fin, but these were removed as they caused the lovable Charlie to look a bit ferocious. He was also given a distinctive voice, which, for the majority of the first 20 years, was supplied by actor Herschel Bernardi of *Fiddler on the Roof* fame.

Charlie has one goal in life – to become a StarKist tuna. To this end, Charlie schemes to convince StarKist that he has "good taste." Charlie reads poetry, plays tennis with an octopus, and does ballet. (*"It looks stupid, but if you do it on tip toes it is interpretive dancing and reveals your good taste to all."*) Charlie always ignores the advice of his sea-world friends – *"Charlie, StarKist doesn't want tuna with good taste, StarKist wants tuna that tastes good!"* Once Charlie even enlisted a gangster fish named Augie, whose intention was to "lean on" StarKist on Charlie's behalf. Of course, Charlie innocently thought of Augie as just what he claimed to be, "a negotiator from out of town."

Consumers identify with Charlie as a guy who never quite made it, and at the same time, admire his indomitable spirit in trying again and again to convince StarKist that he is their kind of tuna. In a counter-intuitive way, Charlie represents StarKist's commitment to superior quality. Over the years, Charlie's character has gradually evolved from its original focus to include a variety of contemporary marketing initiatives. His fans look forward to seeing what Charlie will try next before receiving StarKist's inevitable message – a note dangling from a fish hook that reads, *"Sorry, Charlie."*

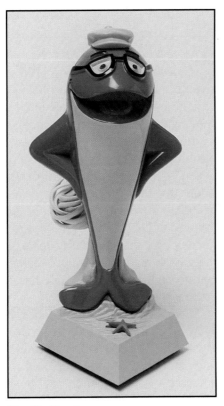

Charlie The Tuna
StarKist Foods, Inc., canned tuna. Plastic telephone, c. 1980s, 10". $40.00.

Charlie The Tuna
StarKist Foods, Inc., canned tuna. Ceramic bank, 1988, 9½". $35.00.

Charlie The Tuna
StarKist Foods, Inc., canned tuna. Vinyl squeeze toy, 1973, 7½". $50.00.

Charlie The Tuna
StarKist Foods, Inc., canned tuna. Plastic transistor AM radio, 1970, 6". $65.00.

Elsie and Elmer   Borden Inc.

Elsie made her first appearance in 1936 as just another pretty cow, in a series of Borden medical journal print ads. Featured along with a variety of cartoon cows named Bessie, Clara, and Mrs. Blossom, Elsie extolled the purity of Borden's milk. When similar commercial ads were run on local network radio, Elsie's amusing spots became so popular that Borden singled her out as its one and only "spokescow." By 1939, she had made her national debut in consumer magazines and Borden's milk bottle caps.

Elsie's "live" career began that same year at the New York World's Fair. In keeping with the Fair's theme, Borden built a futuristic agricultural exhibit, and trained its hostesses to answer scientific questions. To its surprise, the most frequently asked question by the public was, "Which cow is Elsie?" Since Borden wasn't about to disappoint Elsie's admirers, it selected the most beautiful of its cows, a 7-year old, blue-blooded Jersey named "You'll Do Lobelia." For the rest of the season, this particular Elsie, dressed in a beautiful green blanket embroidered with her name, was placed front and center for all to see. And millions did!

There had been no time to design a special setting for Elsie during the Fair's first season. However, in 1940, Borden decided to star Elsie in her own "bovine boudoir," complete with whimsical "Barn Colonial" furniture and props. Before long, Hollywood came calling, offering Elsie a co-starring role in the RKO movie, *Little Men*. As the fabulously successful World Fair exhibit could hardly be left without its star, Borden invented Elsie's husband, Elmer, to take her place. And overnight, the boudoir was disarranged into a summer bachelor pad, strewn with Elmer's red underwear and the remains of nightly poker parties. When Elsie returned for the close of the Fair, she brought along her first offspring, the baby Beulah. When the Fair ended, the Borden's exhibit had outdrawn every other exhibit for the year, including General Motor's multimillion-dollar Futurama.

By 1941, Elsie's cartoon print ad depictions had given up all pretense of her being just an extraordinary, four-legged cow. Since she could already talk, she might as well stand up too. She became a happy mixture of cow and the average American housewife. Although her early ads dealt strictly with milk, Elsie began to promote all of Borden's dairy products. About this time, Borden's chemical division asked to use Elsie for its new white glue product. Since the thought of Elsie as a possible source of the glue was too much for the advertising department (even though the glue is made from milk), Elmer was loaned, as a compromise, for the job. He has been working for Elmer's Glue ever since.

Over the next three decades, Elsie's beautifully illustrated print ads and live tours kept her legend alive. She helped sell war bonds, appeared on television's *What's My Line*, and received honorary university degrees, such as Doctor of Bovinity. In 1947, she gave birth to a calf. A contest to name the new baby brought in one million entries. The judges picked Beauregard, in honor of General Beauregard's association with Bull Run. The promotion was so successful that in 1957 another contest to name her new twins brought in three million suggestions, of which Larabee and Lobelia were selected.

Even with Elsie's tremendous folksy appeal, she was never quite able to make the transition to TV, and she was retired in the late 1960s. Except for occasional promotional appearances, she can still be seen in the famous "Elsie Daisy" logo on cans and packages of Borden's milk and ice cream.

Elsie
The Borden Company, dairy products. Wooden and paper push puppet, "moos" when pressed, c. 1950s, 5". $150.00.

Elsie
Borden, Inc., dairy products. Composition store display, c. 1950s, 10". $400.00.

Elsie
Borden, Inc., dairy products. Ceramic salt and pepper shakers, c. 1950s, 4". $100.00 set.

Beauregard
Borden, Inc., dairy products. Plastic rattle toy, c. 1950s, 5". $35.00.

Elmer
The Borden Chemical Company, A Division of the Borden Company, Elmer's Glue-All. Plastic container, c. 1960s, 6½". $55.00.

Elsie
Borden, Inc., dairy products. Molded vinyl bank, c. 1970s, 9". $115.00.

Little Oscar   Oscar Mayer Foods Inc.

Little Oscar, "the world's smallest chef," was brought to life from an advertising cartoon character in 1936. The first Little Oscar stood approximately 13-wieners tall (i.e., 4 feet, 6 inches). In that same year, Oscar Mayer built a sausage-shaped Wienermobile to take Little Oscar to his various appointments. The company notes that a Wiener-scooter was also considered.

The first Wienermobile, probably one of the most streamlined vehicles of its day, immediately caught the fancy of crowds wherever it went. As newer models of the Wienermobile toured the streets of America, Little Oscar continued to hand out thousands of Wiener Whistles. The Wienermobiles were taken off

the roads in the mid-1970s, and the last Little Oscar retired in the mid-1980s. In 1986, the last drivable Wienermobile from the 1950s' fleet went out on a 50th Anniversary tour. Response to that tour was so overwhelming that the company decided to build six new vehicles, at a cost of $75,000 each. Oscar would have relished the current Wienermobile, which accelerates from 0 to 60 mph in 25 seconds. Its accessories include a sunroof, refrigerator, microwave, and a steamer system that emits the aroma of hot dogs.

Little Oscar in Wienermobile
Oscar Mayer Foods Corporation, wieners and cold cuts. Plastic pull toy, c. 1950s, 4½". At right is a close-up of Little Oscar. $115.00.

Poppin' Fresh, The Pillsbury Doughboy   The Pillsbury Company

For years, the friendly, but bashful, Doughboy has always been eager to help around the kitchen. His only change in temperament came in a 1988 *Wall Street Journal* ad, when he donned boxing gloves to show that Pillsbury was fighting mad about an attempted hostile takeover. Recently, Pillsbury has revamped the image of the Doughboy to celebrate his 25th anniversary. In addition to doing the hokey pokey, he now sings rap songs and plays a butter-knife guitar – a far cry from the simple two-step he performed when he first popped out of a tube of Pillsbury Crescent dinner rolls.

In 1960, the Leo Burnett ad agency landed the refrigerated-dough business from Pillsbury. In those days, the directions on the package advised the consumer to hit the cardboard tube against the edge of a counter to break the package open. Rudi Perz, then working at the agency, wondered, "Wouldn't it be great if someone made of dough popped out of the package?" When Perz drew his first Doughboy, he looked an awful lot like Casper, the Friendly Ghost. Eventually, the Doughboy was shaped into the pudgy, "Poppin' Fresh" character we love today.

The Doughboy has a distinctive giggle which accompanies the traditional poke in the belly he receives at the end of each commercial – although he does not have a belly button! His giggle was performed for 20 years by Paul Frees, who also did the voice for Boris Badenov of the Bullwinkle cartoons. When Frees died, the company undertook a national search to find a comparable giggle.

In 1972, Poppin' Fresh got a mate named Poppie Fresh. In fact, the company licensed a whole family of doughy character premiums, including the Doughboy's eccentric Uncle Rollie. Although Poppie still exists, the loafsome couple has rarely appeared together on company commercials.

Poppin' Fresh
The Pillsbury Company, ready-to-bake dough products. Plastic telephone, c. 1980s, 14". $235.00.

Poppin' Fresh
The Pillsbury Company, ready-to-bake dough products. Molded vinyl squeeze toy, c. 1970s, 6½". $5.00.

Poppin' Fresh
The Pillsbury Company, ready-to-bake dough products. Ceramic bank, 1987, 7½". $40.00.

Poppin' Fresh
The Pillsbury Company, ready-to-bake dough products. Ceramic salt and pepper shakers, c. 1980s, 3½". $30.00 set.

Other Food Products

Aunt Jemima and Uncle Mose
The Quaker Oats Company, Aunt Jemima pancake mix and syrup. Plastic salt and pepper shakers, 1951, 5½". $35.00.

Archie Archway
Archway Food Services. Composition statuette (merit award), c. 1970s, 5". $125.00.

Beefy Frank (left)
Kahn's Wieners, frankfurters. Plastic mustard dispenser, c. 1980s, 5½". $25.00.

Bertolli Chef (right)
Bertolli, Inc., olive oil. Composition statuette and toothpick holder, c. 1950s, 6". $40.00.

Flipje
Koninklijke Mij De Betuwe B.V. (Holland), Betuwe jams and jellies. Plastic key chain, c. 1960s, 2½". $25.00.

Fred Flour
Spillers (England), flour products. Plastic salt and pepper shakers, 1979, 4". $35.00 set.

Gollywogg
James Robertson & Sons (England), Robertson's marmalades and jams. Celluloid store display, c. 1960s, 6". $125.00. Plastic egg cup, c. 1960s, 2". $45.00.

Helping Hand
General Mills, Inc., Hamburger Helper products. Left photo: Plastic transistor AM radio, c. 1980s, 6½". $40.00.
Right photo: Plastic clock, c. 1980s, 6". $40.00.

Marty Mayrose (Butcher)
Swift and Company, Mayrose bacon.
Molded vinyl squeeze toy, 1973, 7½".
$125.00.

Mr. Big Bite
7-Eleven, Big Bite Hot Dogs promotion. PVC figurines, 1989, 4". $10.00 each.

Mr. Tony (left)
Tony's Pizza Service, Tony's "The World's Best" Frozen Pizza. Molded vinyl squeeze toy, 1974, 8½". $40.00.

Wizard of O's (right)
Campbell Soup Company, Franco-American Spaghetti O's. Molded vinyl squeeze toy, 1978, 7½". $15.00.

Swanson Penguin
C.A. Swanson and Sons, frozen TV dinners. Brass statuette, c. 1970s, 4½". $85.00.

Tillie from Tillamook
Tillamook Cheese Company, dairy products. Rubber squeak toy, 1958, 6½". $70.00.

Pet and Livestock Food

Ken-L-Ration Dog
The Quaker Oats Company, Ken-L-Ration dog food. Plastic creamer and salt shaker, c. 1950s, 3". Creamer – $35.00; Salt and pepper shaker set – $15.00.

Hartz Cat and Dog
The Hartz Mountain Corporation, pet food and supplies. Molded vinyl pet toy, c. 1970s, 5". Cat - $40.00; dog - $25.00.

Ernie Pig
G.T.A. Feeds, Lit-O-Bit farm feeds. Ceramic bank, c. 1970s, 8". $165.00.

Meow Mix Cat
Ralston Purina Company, Meow Mix cat food. Molded vinyl pet toy, 1976, 5". $30.00.

Chapter 5
SNACKS AND DESSERTS

Mr. Peanut Planters Lifesavers Company

MR.
PEANUT
®

Mr. Peanut
Standard Brands, Inc., Planter Peanuts. Plastic peanut butter maker, c. 1970s, 12½". $20.00.

Italian immigrant Amedeo Obici, at the age of 19, opened his own fruit stand in Wilkes-Barre, Pennsylvania. Thanks to a $4.50 investment in a peanut roaster, his was a fruit stand with a difference. In those days, roasters had to be continuously turned by hand to keep the peanuts from burning, but the young Obici fixed his so that it would turn automatically. By 1906, sales of these roasted nuts were so successful that Obici abandoned fruits entirely, forming a partnership with his brother-in-law in a new firm called Planters Nut and Chocolate Company.

The company prospered and grew, spurred in part by innovations such as see-through peanut bags. In 1916, Planters offered a prize for the best sketch suitable for adaptation as the company's trademark. A 14-year old schoolboy won the contest with his drawing of an extremely personable peanut. A commercial artist hired to polish the concept added a top hat, monocle, and cane. With its symbol firmly in hand, Planters took out a full-page spread in the *Saturday Evening Post*. This made the product the first salted peanut to be nationally advertised and introduced Mr. Peanut as one of the world's best-known advertising characters.

Mr. Peanut
Nabisco Brands, Inc., Planters Peanuts. Plastic banks, c. 1970s – present, 8½". $10.00 each.

Mr. Peanut
Standard Brands, Inc., Planters Peanuts. Papier maché bobbin' head, c. 1960s, 7". $185.00.

Mr. Peanut
Standard Brands, Inc., Planters Peanuts. Plastic salt and pepper shakers, c. 1950s, 4". $20.00.

Mr. Peanut
Planters Lifesavers Company, Planters Peanuts.
Left: Plastic bank, 1990, 9". $20.00. Right: Mr.
Peanut bendable figure, 1991, 6". $5.00
Nabisco Brands, Inc., Planter Peanuts. Center:
Plastic wind-up walker, 1984, 3". $45.00.

The Sunshine Baker Sunshine Biscuits, Inc. ─────

Sunshine®
Cookies & Crackers

Sunshine Biscuits, Inc. was founded in 1902 by a pair of brothers from Kansas City. The Loose brothers began baking biscuits in above-ground, sunshine-filled bakeries, while the majority of bakeries of the day were confined to dark, basement quarters. Because the Loose Bakeries were so filled with sunshine, the name of Sunshine Biscuits was eventually adopted for its products. In 1908, Sunshine developed a creme-filled sandwich cookie that was to become a big hit. They were looking for a name that would go well with Sunshine. They thought of water because water and Sunshine are elements of purity and cleanliness. Water being a combination of hydrogen and oxygen, they were eager to derive a name from those two words. They combined and abbreviated them, and thus was born HYDROX® Creme Filled

Chocolate Sandwich cookies. By 1912, business was booming, and Sunshine built the famous Thousand Window Bakery in Long Island City, just across the river from New York City. This bakery stood as the largest in the world until the mid-1950s, and the Sunshine Biscuits' sign atop the building grew to be a well-known New York City landmark.

The Sunshine Bakerman character has appeared prominently in many of Sunshine Biscuits' print ads since the 1920s. Using idyllic imagery, past ads relate a day in the life of the Sunshine Bakers:

"At 2 am, our bakers go to knead the dough… Only the moon peeps into the Thousand Window Bakery, …but Sunshine is already there, …Sunshine Bakers whistling cheerily over huge batches of dough. Upon the top floors, Sunshine ovens do their work, above the dirt and dust of traffic."

Although the Thousand Window Bakery has closed, and a new bakery was created in Sayreville, New Jersey in 1964, the Sunshine Baker logo and the popular red-on-yellow graphics of Sunshine products are still among the most recognizable of consumer packaged goods.

Sunshine Bakers
Sunshine Biscuits, Inc., bakery goods. Ceramic salt and pepper shakers, c. 1960s, 2½". $20.00 set.

Other Snack and Dessert Products

Brownie
Girl Scouts of America, Girl Scout Cookies. Ceramic store display, c. 1960s, 7". $20.00.

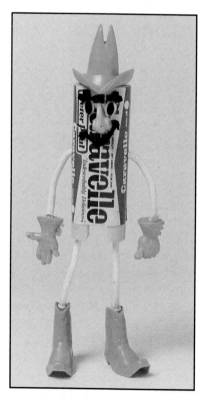

Caravelle Bar
Peter Paul Company, Caravelle candy bars. Paper, wood, plastic toy, 1967, 7½". (Plastic horse not shown.) $125.00.

Choco Late Mousse
Chewie Newgett Company, chocolate candy. Ceramic statuette, 1984, 5". $45.00.

Clark Bar Boy
Beatrice Foods Company, Clark Bar candy. Molded vinyl squeeze toy, c. 1960s, 8½". $225.00.

Ernie, The Keebler Elf
Keebler Company, cookies and baked goods. Molded vinyl squeeze toy, 1974, 7". $15.00.

Fruit Stripe Gum Man
Beech-Nut, Inc., Fruit Stripe Gum. Paper, wood, plastic toy, 1967, 7½". (Plastic motorcycle not shown.) $135.00.

Good Humor Bar
Good Humor Corporation, ice cream. Molded vinyl squeeze toy, 1975, 8". $450.00.

Good Humor Man and Truck
Good Humor Corporation, ice cream bars. Lithographic tin truck, 1950s, 2". $175.00.

Hershey Bar and Hersheykins
Hershey's, chocolate bars and candy. PVC bendable figure, c. 1980s, 4½". $7.00. PVC figurines, c. 1980s, 2". $5.00 each.

Jell-O Baby
General Foods Corporation, Jell-O Gelatin dessert.
Sebastian miniature, 1952, 3½". $450.00.

King Royal
Royal Desserts, Royal Gelatin dessert.
Molded vinyl bank, c. 1970s, 10". $125.00.

M & M's
Mars, Inc., M & M's plain and peanut chocolate candies. Plastic Christmas ornament and package lid, c. 1980s, 2½".
$2.00 each.

M & M's
Mars, Inc., M & M's plain and peanut chocolate candies. PVC keychain ornament, 4", c. 1980s. $3.00 each.

Milton The Toaster
Kellogg Company, Pop-Tarts brand toaster pastries. Plastic and paper bank, 1980, 5". $80.00.

Mr. Wiggle
General Foods Corporation, Jell-O Gelatin dessert. Rubber hand puppet, 1966, 6". $150.00.

Twinkie The Kid
Continental Baking Company, Hostess Twinkies. Composition statue, c. 1980s, 19". $1,850.00.

Chapter 6

BEVERAGES

Fresh-Up Freddie   The Seven-Up Company

"Fresh-Up Freddie"
is a trademark
identifying products of
The Seven-Up Company, 1957.

Fresh-Up Freddie
The Seven-Up Company, 7 UP soda. Molded vinyl squeeze toy, 1959, 9". $250.00.

Fresh-Up Freddie was Walt Disney's first venture into animated, television commercials. In 1957, The Seven-Up Company met with Disney to select an advertising figure from the studio's vast collection of cartoon characters. A bright and bubbly rooster was chosen and named Freddie, supposedly in honor of a Seven-Up bottler, Fred Lutz, Jr. Freddie was modeled after the rooster, Pancuito, from the Disney movie, *Three Caballeros*. But Freddie was a lot smarter and the personification of Seven-Up's happy slogan – "You like it. It likes you!"

By 1958, Freddie made his debut in the popular, Disney-produced television show, *Zorro*. Freddie's Seven-Up commercials were classic Disney, beautifully animated and full of gags. The ebullient Freddie gave tips on how to entertain friends with, of course, his favorite drink, 7 UP. Although Freddie was the life of the party, he was not ashamed to resort to his "shelf of laughs" containing jars of "Chuckles," "Giggles," and incredibly hysterical "Ha-Ha's."

Funny Face   Brady Enterprises, Inc.

"FUNNY FACE"®

Funny Face powdered, fruit-flavored drink mixes burst onto the market in 1965. It was Pillsbury's attempt to siphon off some business from its chief competitor, General Mills' successful Kool-Aid. Both products were quite similar in packaging and ingredients. So to compete with Kool-Aid's Smiling Face Pitcher, Pillsbury came up with not one, but a whole family of advertising characters – one for each flavor. There was Rootin'-Tootin' Raspberry, Freckle Face Strawberry, Goofy Grape, Ruddi Tutti-Frutti, Loud Mouth Punch, "With It" Watermelon, and Lefty Lemonade. Two of the first characters were introduced as ethnic characters, Injun Orange and Chinese Cherry, but the company prudently reissued them as Jolly Olly Orange and Choo Choo Cherry.

The incredibly popular Funny Face characters were issued as premiums in the form of walkers, drinking mugs, and pitchers. Although consumers loved the fruity faces, the drink never achieved the market share that Pillsbury had hoped. In 1980, the rights to "Funny Face" were sold to Brady Enterprises, a New England company. Seven flavors of Funny Face drink mixes are still marketed by Brady on the Eastern Seaboard.

Choo Choo Cherry, Jolly Olly Orange, Goofy Grape, Rootin'-Tootin' Raspberry
The Pillsbury Company, Funny Face fruit-flavored drink mixes. Plastic walkers (weights not depicted), c. 1970s, 3". $45.00 each.

Punchy   Hawaiian Punch, Procter & Gamble

"Hey! How about a nice Hawaiian Punch?"

"Sure," says the ever-gullible Oaf, who then gets decked by the pugilistic Punchy.

As soon as this first Hawaiian Punch cartoon commercial appeared on Jack Paar's, *The Tonight Show,* in 1963, Punchy and the Oaf became a knockout hit. In fact, Paar took one look at it and said, "Let's run that again!" Fruit Juicy Red Hawaiian Punch was on its way to becoming the largest selling, ready-to-drink, noncarbonated soft drink in the nation. Over the next three decades, a series of commercials chronicled the antics of Punchy and the tourist-garbed Oaf, always ending with Punchy's slapstick, roundhouse blow.

Like many famous spokespersons, Punchy has experienced career ups and downs. In 1966, Punchy paired with a Hula girl. Since she attracted more attention to herself than to Hawaiian Punch, Punchy reclaimed headliner status two years later. Again, in

the 1970s, his role was reduced when Donny and Marie Osmond played the lead in Hawaiian Punch commercials, leaving Punchy only a supporting role at the end of each segment. He remained in semi-retirement until 1988, when Hawaiian Punch, in celebration of Punchy's 25th anniversary as company spokesman, reintroduced him as "the best salesman the brand has ever had."

Punchy
Del Monte USA, Hawaiian Punch drink. Plastic telephone, c. 1980s, 11". $150.00.

Punchy
RJR Foods, Hawaiian Punch drink. Plastic game pieces, 1976, 3". $15.00 set.

Harry Hood
H.P. Hood, Inc., dairy products and orange juice. Sebastian miniature, 1983, 5". $400.00.

Harry Hood
H.P. Hood, Inc., dairy products and orange juice. Molded vinyl squeeze toy, c. 1970s, 7½". $70.00.

ICEE Bear
ICEE Developers, Inc., crushed ice soft drink. Molded vinyl bank, c. 1970s, 8". $30.00.

Dancin' Kool-Aid Man (left)
Kraft General Foods, Inc., Kool-Aid brand soft drink mix. Sound-activated dancing vinyl statuette, 1991, 9". $35.00.

Kool-Aid Pitcher (right)
General Foods Corporation, Kool-Aid soft drink mix. Plastic mechanical bank, c. 1970s, 7". $25.00.

Kleek-O
Cliquot Club, ginger ale soda. Ceramic bank, c. 1930s, 5". $185.00.

Luzianne Mammy
Wm. B. Reily & Company, Inc., Luzianne Coffee. Plastic salt and pepper shakers, c. 1950s, 5½". (Green striped shakers were a licensed premium. Red shakers were a novelty item.) Green – $125.00 set; Red – $20.00 set.

Lucky Lymon
The Coca-Cola Company, Sprite soda. Molded vinyl talking doll, 1990, 7½". $20.00.

Max Headroom
The Coca-Cola Company, Coca-Cola soda. Plastic candy container, 1987, 2½". $5.00.

Quik Bunny
Nestlé Food Corporation, Nestlé Quik. PVC
figurine, 1991, 6". $5.00.

Quik Bunny
Nestlé Food Corporation, Nestlé Quik. Plastic mug, c. 1980s, 4½". $7.50.
Chocolate syrup container, c. 1980s, 8½". $5.00.

Squirt
The Squirt Company, Squirt soda. Ceramic bank, 1948, 8". $275.00.

Squirt
The Squirt Company, Squirt soda. Composition store display, 1947, 13". $450.00.

Tang Lips
General Foods Corporation, Tang Breakfast Beverage Crystals. PVC figures, c. 1980s, 3". $2.00 each.

Chapter 7
BEER AND LIQUOR

Bert and Harry Piel Piel Bros. Brewing Company

Although the product they peddled was never sold beyond a few hundred miles of New York City, and they never appeared on anything other than local radio or television, Bert and Harry Piel attained national fame and became advertising classics in the 1950s.

The soft-spoken, modest Harry and the overblown Bert were the fictitious owners of the Piel Bros. Brewing Company. They were played by Bob Elliot and Ray Goulding of the incomparable comedy team, Bob and Ray. Their radio and animated television spots grew so popular that television sections in newspapers began listing when the commercials would appear on the evening schedule.

The garrulous Bert spent most of his time creating offbeat, but flawed, advertising gimmicks, while the reserved Harry was more concerned with producing a better beer and getting this message to the public. One irreverent commercial found Bert announcing the winner of the employee contest to name a new slogan, which he claims *"was Harry's idea to build spirit. Make them think working is fun."* The top entry: "Piel's, the beer with the barrel of flavor." *"What's his name will get a kick out of hearing his name on radio,"* Bert commented.

Another spot depicted the brothers at a bowling alley. Bert unashamedly advised, *"If you enjoy bowling, sip Piel's between every frame. Don't worry about your score, the main thing is to enjoy yourself."* When the characters were retired in 1960, New Yorkers so grieved their absence that Piel's brought them back for several more years of brewery antics. Piel's Brand Beer is now sold in 13 states and several foreign countries.

Bert and Harry Piel
Piel Bros. Brewing Company, Piel's Beer. Painted metal statuette, 1956, 9". $75.00. (Wooden beer mug rack not shown.)

Bert and Harry Piel
Piel Bros. Brewing Company, Piel's Beer. Ceramic salt and pepper shakers, c. 1950s, 3" and 4". $135.00 set.

Bert and Harry Piel
Piel Bros. Brewing Company, Piel's Beer. Molded vinyl store display, 1963, 11½". $95.00.

Hamm's Bear   Pabst Brewing Company

In the early 1950s, the Minnesota-based Hamm's Brewery promoted its Hamm's Beer with the slogan, "From the Land of Sky Blue Waters." The motifs of cool, refreshing northern lakes and tom-tom music proved to be quite successful. After several years, however, the campaign's creator, the advertising agency, Campbell-Mithun, had begun to feel restless with the concept; something new and vibrant was needed. That something was the Hamm's Bear, a goofy, bumbling cartoon figure, with whom Hamm's Beer would be forever linked.

The Hamm's Bear was a bit inept and clumsy but always good-natured and sincere. He had many woodland friends to play with, and several rivals, such as the Fox and Beavers. The northland setting and emphasis on sports made for prizewinning commercials and wide-audience appeal. In the spot "Hockey Bear" (1958), the Bear stars as the goalie for the Hamm's All Stars. As two beavers chew off part of his hockey stick, he stops the Fox from scoring, to the crowd's adulation. He catches the Wolf's next hard shot in his mouth, throwing him into the net for the score. As was the case in many commercials, momentary triumph could easily be turned into comical defeat for the Hamm's Bear.

As the popularity of the Bear increased, Hamm's began using him in point-of-purchase promotions. These "stackers," as they came to be known, were figural bears in amusing poses, placed on poles and stuck into stacks of beer cartons. They have since become some of the most sought-after of Hamm's collectibles.

By 1969, the brewery was owned by Heublein, Inc. Its new ad agency was tired of the Bear and sent him into hibernation. He resurfaced in 1972 as a new persona, Theodore H. Bear, a more serious, take-charge spokesman, donning a blazer and tie. When this campaign foundered, out went T. H. and in came Sasha, a live, Kodiak bear, who ambled through the wilderness with a curly-haired woodsman known as the Hamm's Man. Although Sasha and the Hamm's Man lasted longer than did the brewery management at that time, they could not capture the nostalgic appeal of the early Bear commercials. The brewery was eventually taken over by Olympia, and then Pabst, in the late 1970s and 1980s. Since then, the cartoon Hamm's Bear has returned, a bit older and flabbier, to the delight of his fans.

Hamm's Bear
Theo. Hamm Brewing Company, Hamm's Beer. Ceramic salt and pepper shakers, c. 1980s, 6". $35.00 set.

Hamm's Bear
Theo. Hamm Brewing Company, Hamm's Beer. Vacuum plastic store display, c. 1960s, 9". $55.00. (Only portion of display is shown.)

Hamm's Bear
Pabst Brewing Company, Hamm's Beer. Ceramic bank, c. 1980s, 11". $35.00.

Spuds MacKenzie   Anheuser-Busch, Inc.

Spuds MacKenzie's ascent to stardom began in 1983. At the time, Bud Light Beer sales were languishing behind its chief competitor. In an effort to attract young adults, the ad agency, DDB Needham, introduced Spuds, "The Original Bud Light Party Animal."

This "Ayatollah of Party-ola" was a rakish bull terrier, accompanied by his adoring human friends – the "Spudettes." After appearing on a poster and calendar, Spuds was successfully testmarketed in California. His prime-time national debut, the 1987 Super Bowl, was a smash. Spuds quickly became one of the most successful advertising phenomena of the 1980s, as Bud Light sales soared.

In his many commercials, Spuds travels the fast lane, benignly supervising the exciting activities around him. He does his own stunts, except when he refused to dive into a pool and had to be replaced by a stunt dog. And in a ski-jumping spot aired during the Calgary Olympics, a stuffed stand-in was used. In recent years, Spuds' message of moderation, "It's cool to know when to say when," reflects the company's cooperation with alcohol-awareness groups.

Research showed that the suave, jet-set Spuds was viewed by women as cute and adorable, and by men as "living the good life" – lolling at beaches, yachting, and associating with beautiful women. Spuds is now in retirement and is no longer used in Bud Light's marketing efforts. But the memory of Spuds lives on. And, by the way, the real life Spuds is actually a she!

Spuds MacKenzie
Anheuser-Busch, Inc., Bud Light Beer. Composition statuette, c. 1980s, 6½". $250.00.

Spuds MacKenzie
Anheuser-Busch, Inc., Bud Light Beer. Polyethylene store display light, c. 1980s, 15". $100.00.

Other Liquor Products

Big "D"
Drewry's Brewing Company, Drewry's Beer. Plastic store display (base not shown), 1957, 8". Without base – $55.00; With base – $145.00.

Blatz Baseball Players
Blatz Brewing Company, Blatz Beer. Metal store display, 1968, 16". $185.00.

Blatz Beer Men

Blatz Brewing Company, Blatz Beer. Metal can and glass bottle store display, 1968, 11" and 14". $85.00 each.

Blatz Beer Man

Blatz Brewing Company, Blatz Beer. Plastic store display, 1960, 12". $55.00. (Detail of metal store display.)

Blue Nun ("Correct with any dish")

H. Sichel Söhne, GMBH Weinkellerer (Germany), Blue Nun wines. Ceramic salt and pepper shakers, c. 1970s, 4½". $175.00 set.

Blue Nun
H. Sichel Söhne, GMBH Weinkellerer (Germany), Blue Nun wines. Vinyl store display, 1974, 12" (base not depicted.) Without base – $40.00; With base – $75.00.

Bud Man
Anheuser-Busch, Inc., Budweiser Beer. Molded vinyl tab knob, 1991, 9". $65.00.

Bud Man
Anheuser-Busch, Inc., Budweiser Beer. Ceramic beer stein, 1989, 8½". $30.00.

Burgie!
Burgermeister Brewing Corporation, Burgie Beer. Detail of metal store display, c. 1970s, 14". $75.00.

Burgie!
Burgermeister Brewing Corporation, Burgie Beer. Plastic store display, c. 1970s, 10". $65.00.

Colonel Glenmore
Glenmore Distilleries Company, whiskey. Plaster ashtray, c. 1960s, 3½". $40.00.

Coronet Waiter
Cresta Blanca Wine Company, Coronet VSQ Brandy. Composition store displays, c. 1950s, 19". $185.00.

Coronet Waiter
Cresta Blanca Wine Company, Coronet VSQ Brandy. Plastic and cork bottle spout, c. 1950s, 3½". $30.00.

Dancing Russian
Nikolai Vodka, vodka. Plaster statuette, c. 1970s, 12".
$75.00.

Falls City Bottleman
Falls City Brewing Company, Falls City Beer.
Composition nodder, 1970, 14". $150.00.

Foremost Bottle
Foremost Sales Promotions, beverage and bottle shops.
Plaster bank, c. 1970s, 7". $85.00.

Johnnie Pfeiffer
Pfeiffer's, Pfeiffer's Beer. Painted plaster store display, 1952, 8". $45.00.

Johnnie Walker
John Walker & Sons/Canada Dry Corporation, blended Scotch whiskey. Composition store display, c. 1950s, 15". $35.00.

"My Goodness – My Guinness"
Arthur Guinness Son & Company, Guinness Stout. Carlton Ware statuettes, 1955, 3½". $45.00 each.

Oertel's '92 Man
Oertel Brewing Company, Oertel's '92 Beer. Plaster store display, 1954, 15". $225.00.

Pedrito
Canada Dry Corporation, Canada Dry mixers. Wooden statuette with pop-up hat marked "Olé!", c. 1970s, 7". $95.00.

Old Crow (left)
W.A. Gaines and Company, Old Crow Whiskey. Plastic store display, c. 1960s, 5½". $15.00.

Suntory Gangster (center)
Suntory Ltd., Suntory Whiskey. Plastic toothpick holder, c. 1980s, 4". $75.00.

Monte Téca "Try Me" (right)
Monte Téca, liqueur made with tequila. Plastic wind-up walker, c. 1980s, 3". $25.00.

Rainier Waiter
Rainier Brewing Company, Rainier Beer. Plaster statuette, 1956, 6½". $175.00.

Rainier Brewer
Rainier Brewing Company, Rainier Beer. Papier maché store display bobbin' head, 1955, 16". $150.00.

Dino
Sinclair Oil Corporation, gasoline service stations. Plastic bank, c. 1960s, 4". $25.00.

Dinoland Dino
Sinclair Oil Corporation, gasoline service stations. New York World's Fair wax statuette, 4½",1964. $25.00. Soap, 1964, 3½". $17.50.

The Esso Oildrop   Exxon Corporation

The Esso Oildrop was first developed by Esso's Danish company during World War II to explain the reason behind war shortages of petroleum products. Before long, the little guy achieved a fame all his own and was adapted by Esso's other European affiliates. In Switzerland, he was known as "Quibibb Esso."

The Esso Oildrop made his United States debut in 1958 for Standard Oil. At that time, Esso's successful trademark slogan was "Happy Motoring." Although he appeared in many of the company's publications and advertisements, he became best known for his travel-related activities on Esso's service station maps. The Oildrop's popularity eventually evaporated in 1964 when the Humble Tiger roared to the forefront of Esso's ad campaigns.

Esso Oildrop
Standard Oil Company (Germany), Esso gasoline service stations. Plaster tree ornament, 1961, 3½". $85.00.

Esso Oildrop
Standard Oil Company, Esso gasoline service stations. Cardboard statuette, c. 1960s, 6". $40.00. Plastic bank, c. 1960s, 7". $80.00.

Esso Oildrop (left)
Standard Oil Company, Esso gasoline service stations. Plastic bank, c. 1960s, 7". $95.00.

Esso Oildrop (right)
Standard Oil Company, Esso gasoline service stations. Metal statuette, c. 1960s, 6". $155.00.

The Exxon Tiger Exxon Corporation

Esso's use of the tiger symbol dates back to the turn of the century, when a leaping bengal appeared on roadside pumps in Norway. European affiliates continued to use the tiger in the 1930s and 1950s to promote Esso gasolines. By 1959, the affiliates were no longer using the animal in their ads. But in that same year, the tiger made his United States debut, when a young Chicago copywriter, Emery Smith, strung a few simple words together – "Put a tiger in your tank."

Although the slogan proved successful for Oklahoma Oil Company, it still lacked something. In

1964, Humble Oil, another division of Esso, supplied the missing magic, aided by a few strokes of an artist's brush – the "right" sort of cartoon tiger. Seemingly a close cousin of A. A. Milne's beloved Tigger, the Humble tiger was a friendly, lovable beast, who could also convey the impression of power. In areas where Humble had been wishing its customers "Happy Motoring" for 30 years, the tiger immediately caught the public's fancy.

Humble's marketing division was quick to offer a host of tiger-related premiums, the most memorable of which was a stuffed tiger tail that could be tied onto the trunk of one's car. Sales soared and *Time* magazine dubbed 1964 as "The Year of the Tiger along Madison Avenue."

Spurred by Humble's American success, the company's South American and European affiliates also adopted the tiger, accompanied by such slogans as *"Pack den Tiger in den Tank."* Australia decided to market a raging, ferocious tiger, a departure from his jovial, American counterpart. By 1965, the Australian tiger had been tamed, and he, too, cut a successful advertising swath throughout the Southern hemisphere and the Far East.

Esso's most successful promotional campaigns were losing some gas by the end of the decade and the tiger was retired. When the company changed its name to Exxon in 1972, the tiger was briefly recalled into service. The company claimed, "We're changing our name, but not our stripes." In one memorable, animated commercial, the Tiger received a telegram at the Home for Advertising Characters. "They want me back," he exclaimed as Elsie, Mr. Peanut and a number of other characters wished him well.

In the 1980s, the company again brought back the tiger, but this time in live-action form. He has since been racing up snowy mountains and along sunny beaches to symbolize the power and dependability of Exxon gasoline.

Humble Tiger
Humble Oil and Refining Company, gasoline service stations. Plastic bank, c. 1960s, 8½". $30.00.

The Mack Bulldog Mack Trucks, Inc.

Mack and the bulldog design are registered trademarks of Mack Trucks, Inc.

The heavy-duty Mack AC truck, a hard-tired, chain-driven brute, served the British and American troops during World War I with incredible toughness and dependability. When a lesser truck became stuck, the British would yell "Aye, bring one of those Bulldogs in!" The AC's, with their snub-nosed hood, resembled bulldogs – not only in performance, but also in appearance. Hence they became known as Mack Bulldogs. By 1922, the company adopted the Bulldog as its symbol, incorporating the bulldog in its advertisements and truck name plates.

In 1932, A. F. Masury, Mack's chief engineer, was hospitalized for about a week. At that time, a large soap company was sponsoring a nationwide soap sculpturing contest. The bedridden Masury, a man of action, summoned one of his aides to pick up a case of soap and began carving away. The result was a cubistic rendering of his favorite canine. Whether he actually entered the contest is unclear, however, with his staunch squared lines and rampant pose, Masury's Bulldog had the no-nonsense, ready-to-work look that made him the perfect radiator cap mascot. Cast in metal, the Bulldog has peered from the hood of every Mack truck since.

The world's largest Mack Bulldog can be seen atop the company's headquarters in Allentown, Pennsylvania. He stands without the Mack name beside him. According to the company, the Bulldog says it all.

Mack Bulldog
Mack Trucks, Inc., trucks. Plastic bank, c. 1970s, 8".
$60.00.

Mack Bulldog
Mack Trucks, Inc., trucks. Plastic bank, c. 1970s, 8".
$45.00.

Mack Bulldog
Mack Trucks, Inc., trucks. Metal statuette, c. 1970s,
3". $25.00.

The Michelin Man (Bibendum) Michelin Tire Corporation

The Michelin brothers, André and Edouard, ran a small family business that primarily manufactured rubber products. In 1891, the innovative pair patented an air-filled tire composed of an inner tube that could easily be repaired by removing it from its rim. At that time, most vehicles used solid tires or solid tires with tubes glued to them. These pneumatic Michelins were quite successful, and a year later, 10,000 Frenchmen were using detachable tires on their bicycles.

While walking around the Lyon Exhibition several years later, the Michelin brothers came upon a display of different-sized tires, stacked one on top of another, with the largest ones causing a bulge in the middle. His imagination aroused, Edouard remarked, "Add arms and you've got a man." Four years later, Michelin hired the poster artist, O'Galop, who did exactly that. The Michelin man was born and named "Bibendum."

Why Bibendum? At the time, Michelin's advertising slogan was *"Le Pneu Michelin Boit L'Obstacle"* (Michelin tires swallow up all obstacles.) O'Galop's poster depicted the Michelin Man standing behind a banquet table, huge goblet in hand, offering a toast. In the goblet were a tire's worst enemies – a cocktail of metal nails and shards of glass. As the Michelin Man boastfully proclaims, *"Nunc est bibendum,"* Latin for "Let us drink," two partially deflated, competing tire men cower beside the robust and macho "Bib."

Bibendum, in his early years, wore spectacles and smoked a big, fat cigar. Over the years, the layers of narrow tires have given way to wider ones of more modern appearance. He continues to appear in the company's world-renowned tour guides and tire advertisements. He is most popular with European and Canadian truckers, who affix plastic Bib figures to their cabs. Some even sport them in pairs and light them up at night!

Bibendum
Michelin Tire Corporation, tires. Molded vinyl statuette, c. 1980s, 14". $75.00. Ceramic novelty statuette, c. 1990s, 11". $20.00.

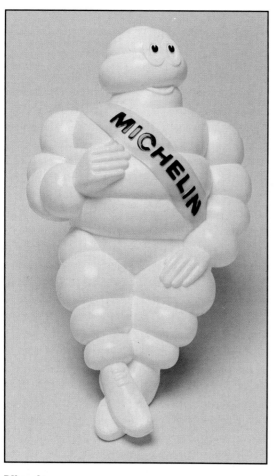

Bibendum
Michelin Tire Corporation, tires. Plastic truck display, c. 1980s, 15". $75.00.

Bibendum
Michelin Tire Corporation, tires. Plastic store display, c. 1980s, 12". $45.00.

Bibendum
Michelin Tire Corporation, tires. Bakelite ashtray, c. 1930s, 4½". $55.00.

Other Automotive Products and Services

Bear

Bear Automotive Service, wheel alignment equipment. Plaster statuettes, c. 1960s, 4". $55.00.

Continental Tire Man

Continental Tires, radial tires. PVC figurine, c. 1980s, 2". $35.00.

Champ Man (left)

Champion Auto Stores, Inc. Home-owned auto parts stores. PVC bendable figure, 1991, 6". $12.50.

Fisk Tire Boy

Uniroyal, Inc., tires. Plastic bank, c. 1970s, 8½". $175.00.

Jaguar
Jaguar, Jaguar licensed products. Wooden store display, c. 1980s, 3". $45.00.

Freddy Fast
Douglas Oil Company, gasoline service stations. Plastic doll, 1976, 7". $55.00.

"KC" Piston
Korody-Colyer Corporation, industrial engine parts. Papier maché bobbin' head, c. 1960s, 7". $200.00.

Micronex Tread Mike
Binney & Smith Company (England), Micronex Tread tires. Rubber and metal cigarette lighter, c. 1940s, 6". $400.00.

Nosey
Standard Oil Company, Esso solvents. Metal statuette, c. 1960s, 5½". $75.00.

Mr. Goodwrench
General Motors Corporation, GM Parts Division. Jim Beam bottle, 1978, 13". $55.00.

Mr. Fleet
Chrysler Corporation, Chrysler automobiles. Molded vinyl bank, 1973, 9½". $275.00.

Pepe Chevron
Chevron Corporation (Mexico), gasoline service stations. Ceramic desk statuette, c. 1980s, 6". $95.00.

Phillips 66 Man
Phillips Petroleum Company, gasoline service stations. Silvered metal statuette, c. 1970s, 3½". $35.00.

Rocky
Rockwell Standard, Transmission and Axle Division. Composition ashtray, c. 1950s, 6". $300.00.

Save With OK
OK Rubber Welders, Autofloat Tires. Plastic bank, c. 1960s, 6". $45.00.

TECH

Chrysler Corporation, Master Technician Service award. Metal statuette with piston base, 1957, 5½". $65.00.

Stopper

American Brake Shoe Company, American Brakeblok safety brake lining. Painted plaster statuette, c. 1970s, 3". $55.00.

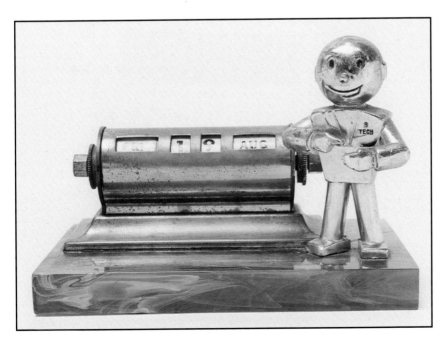

TECH

Chrysler Corporation, Master Technician Service award. Metal statuette desk **calendar**, 1957, 4". $65.00.

TECH

Chrysler Corporation, Master Technician Service award. Metal statuette, 1957, 4". $45.00.

Wise-Buy Owl
Wards Stores, Riverside Tires. Metal bank, 1970s, 6". $40.00. Painted plaster
statuette, 1970s, 5". $45.00.

Chapter 9
APPLIANCES AND EQUIPMENT

The Facit Man   Facit AB

FACIT.

Facit AB is a Swedish maker of adding machines, display terminals, typewriters, and calculators. In the late 1950s, Ivan Hammer, the company's advertising manager, noted that Facit's competitors always stressed the drudgery of figure work in their promotions. "Couldn't the dry and impersonal emphasis be brightened up by something less serious?" he thought. And with this in mind, the Facit Man was born.

The clever little Facit wizard wore a pointed, black thinking cap decorated with numbers. In his hand, he held a wand with which to solve problems. The first Facit Man was an older character, but like many ad characters, became younger looking over the years.

Hammer approached the introduction of his little mascot with some trepidation. "Whoever heard of adopting a light-hearted approach to persuade serious people to buy modern calculators?" he thought. The wizard's first appearance came in the adding machine instruction manuals. Previously, these booklets were solid text, without a single illustration. With the little Facit Man explaining instructions to the reader at strategic points, the manual began to come alive. Things were looking good for the new symbol.

The company then began to use the Facit Man in promotional gifts and showroom displays. A giant-sized wizard was even created for appearances at exhibitions. The mascot was so popular in Europe that over one-million figures were made. The company notes that in the 1960s, at the height of his popularity, several hundred could be found on desks of United Nations officials – the Facit Man acting as a goodwill ambassador that bridged the gap between businessmen of different nations.

Facit Man
Facit AB, adding machines and calculators. Plastic store display, c. 1960s, 22". $350.00.

Nipper
RCA Victor, phonographs and radios. Painted plaster statuette, c. 1980s, 4". $25.00.

Nipper
RCA Victor, phonographs and radios. Chalk statuette, c. 1930s, 3". $35.00.

Other Products

Hoover Housewife
The Hoover Company, Hoover vacuums. Ceramic novelty bobbin' head, c. 1960s, 8". $275.00.

Iron Fireman
Iron Fireman Company, furnances. Metal statuette ashtray, c. 1940s, 5". $55.00.

Lennie Lennox
Lennox Furnace Company, furnaces and heaters. Ceramic bank, 1949, 7½". $225.00. Salt shaker, 1950, 4½". $165.00 set.

Magic Chef (left)
Magic Chef, Inc., gas ranges. Molded vinyl bank, c. 1980s, 7". $10.00.

Magic Chef (right)
Magic Chef, Inc., gas ranges. Ceramic salt shaker, c. 1950s, 5". $90.00 set.

Magic Chef
Magic Chef, Inc., gas ranges. Plastic salt and pepper shakers, c. 1950s, 5". $40.00 set.

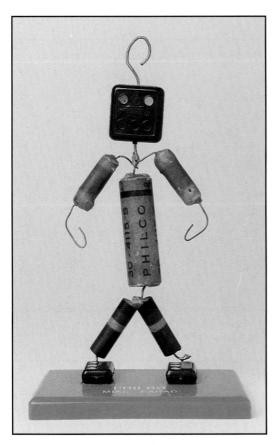

Philco Transistor Man (left)
Philco, transistor radios and hi-fi's. Transistor, plastic, and wood in-house statuette, c. 1960s, 5". $225.00.

Phil Quota (right)
Sears Roebuck and Company, appliances. Plaster statuette (sales award), c. 1950s, 4½". $400.00.

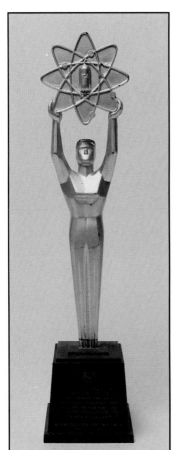

RCA (left)
Radio Corporation of America, Television Service Technician award. Plastic statuette, 1955, 19". $50.00.

Sony Boy (right)
Sony Corporation, televisions, radios, and hi-fi's. Molded vinyl doll, c. 1960s, 4". $225.00.

Tappan Chef
Tappan Appliance Company, ranges and appliances.
Painted plaster statuette, c. 1950s, 8". $75.00.

Tappan Chefs
Tappan Appliance Company, ranges and appliances.
Ceramic salt and pepper shakers, c. 1960s, 4". $25.00.

"TV" Joe
Radio Corporation of America, RCA Silverama tubes. Plastic
bank, 1960, 5". $55.00.

Westinghouse Tuff Guy (1940)
Westinghouse Electric Corporation, appliances and ranges. Composition wood statuette, 1940, 4". $150.00.

Westinghouse Tuff Guy (1952)
Westinghouse Electric Corporation, appliances and ranges. Painted plaster statuette, 1952, 5½". $65.00.

"Your Warm Friend"
Thatcher Company, boilers, ranges, and furnaces. Metal statuette, c. 1920s, 3". $35.00.

Chapter 10

HARDWARE AND HOUSEWARE

Dutch Boy   Dutch Boy Paints

In 1907, The National Lead Company, a consortium of white lead manufacturers, was looking to consolidate its products under one common trademark design. Several years earlier, Rudolf Yook, an illustrator of Dutch ancestry, had drawn several advertisements for the company. Because the people of Holland had a worldwide reputation for keeping their buildings immaculately white-washed, and because the company's white lead paint was made from a famous "Dutch" process, Yook's sketches had featured a little Dutch boy, dressed in native overalls and in the act of painting.

After considering a number of proposed designs, National Lead chose Yook's sketches of the Dutch Boy as the company's new trademark. With this rough concept, the firm then commissioned the noted artist, Lawrence Carmichael Earl, to paint the new symbol's portrait. Earl picked a nine-year-old neighborhood boy, Michael Brady, as his model. The child was asked first to wear his costume of wooden shoes, overalls, and cap for several days so that it would look naturally worn out. As he worked, Earl may have had in mind Gainsborough's masterpiece, "Blue Boy," to which the finished Dutch Boy oil painting was later compared.

The Irish Michael Brady, who soon became America's best-known Dutchman, grew up to be an accomplished political cartoon artist.

Dutch Boy
Dutch Boy Paints, paints. Painted pressed cardboard store display, c. 1950s, 15". $150.00.

Mr. Clean Procter & Gamble

In 1958, Procter & Gamble made its new liquid cleanser a household word in one big, brawny, bald-headed wink – Mr. Clean. At the time, Lestoil was the nation's number-one, all-purpose cleanser. Even before the product formulation was fully developed, Procter & Gamble had come up with the name, Mr. Clean. Through the use of clever, animated commercials, Mr. Clean demonstrated the versatility of the product, together with the jingle:

Mr. Clean will clean your whole house,
And everything that's in it,
Floors, door,
Walls, hall,
White side-wall tires and old golf balls.

Within weeks, viewers all over America were humming the tune. By 1960, Mr. Clean had muscled his way into the number-one cleanser spot until he was swept from first place by Ajax's "White Tornado" several years later.

According to the company, the one-earringed Mr. Clean was probably a sailor. While his attire has typically been strictly all-white sailor scrubs, there was a time when he wore a business suit and tie in some live-action commercials. Mr. Clean was even given a first name when Procter & Gamble held a "Give Mr. Clean a First Name" contest in 1962. Chosen from thousands of entries, the winner was "Veritably."

Through the years, the Mr. Clean character has gotten "tougher," reflecting the product's improved formulations. In 1963, he played a police "grime-fighter," actually arresting dirt problems from his police motorcycle. By 1965, the product was at parity with competing ammoniated-cleansers. To convince the public that Mr. Clean was the product to buy, he got mad at dirt, becoming the "Mean Mr. Clean." Next, he became a two-fisted, "dirt" boxer – knocking out grime with one hand and leaving shine with the other. Additional ad campaigns saw him grow whiskers, gave him a black eye to show off his floor "shiner," and had him testify in court against dirt.

By 1968, Mr. Clean became a "changed man" as the product was reformulated to include a pine aroma. As advertising tastes changed in the late 1960s and through the 1970s, Mr. Clean took a leave of absence, although his smiling face continued to appear on the product label. In celebrating his 25th anniversary, Mr. Clean has since returned to the screen as "The Man behind the Shine." The company notes that he doesn't even have a single gray hair!

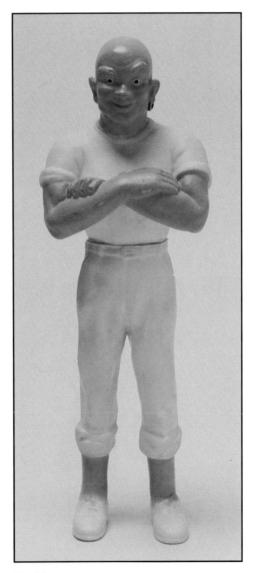

Mr. Clean
Procter & Gamble, Mr. Clean all-purpose cleaner. Vinyl doll, 1961, 8". $85.00.

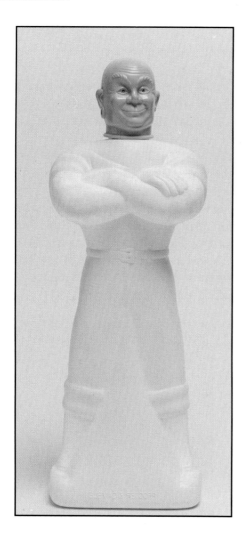

Mr. Clean
Procter & Gamble, Mr. Clean all-purpose cleaner. Plastic bottle, c. 1960s, 12". $175.00.

The Little Man with the Hammer   Western Exterminator Company

In 1931, the telephone company approached the Western Exterminator owners with the idea that advertising in the Yellow Pages would increase sales. It was also suggested that a trademark logo might enhance customer-recognition of Western's name. Thus, from the pen of Vaughn Kaufman, an art department employee for the telephone company, came The Little Man with the Hammer.

The Little Man and the mouse were an immediate success. The top-hatted fellow was once known as "Kernal Kleenup," and later as "Inspector Holmes." But neither of these names ever really caught on with employees, and he is still affectionately referred to as the "Little Man."

Today, he stands 17-feet tall on the roof of Western Exterminator offices in Burlingame and Long Beach, California, raising a warning finger at a little, four-feet tall mouse. In a much smaller version, the Little Man can also be found atop the chemical boxes of every company truck.

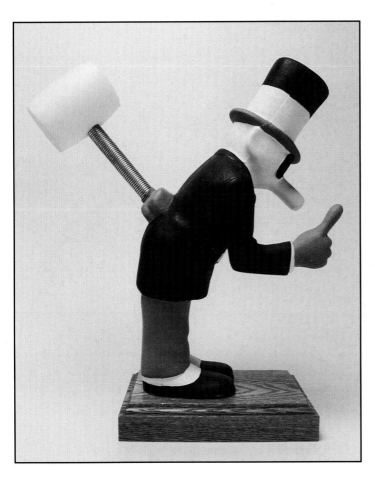

The Little Man with the Hammer
Western Exterminator Company, exterminator services. Composition truck display, c. 1980s, 20". $135.00.

Other Products

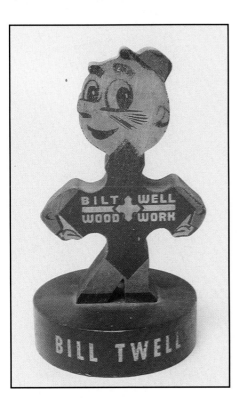

BILL TWELL (left)
Bilt Well, Inc., woodwork services. Wooden statuette, c. 1950s, 5". $275.00.

Chore Boy (right)
Reckitt & Coleman Household Products, Chore Boy brand sponges and scouring pads. Molded vinyl toy, 1991, 6". $25.00.

Energizer Bunny
Eveready Battery Company, Inc., Energizer brand batteries. Molded vinyl squeeze light, 1991, 4½". $10.00.

Eveready Cat
Union Carbide Corporation, Eveready batteries. Plastic bank, c. 1970s, 6". $10.00.

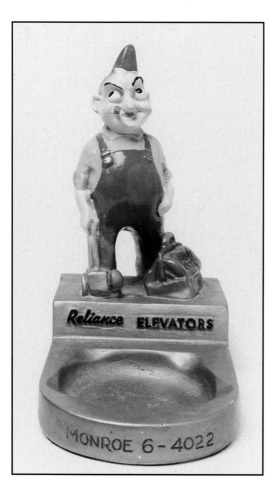

Handy Andy (left)
Reliance Elevators, elevator service and repair. Plaster ashtray, c. 1950s, 7". $400.00.

Happy Homer (right)
Staggs-Bilt Homes, home construction. Papier maché bobbin' head, c. 1960s, 6". $250.00.

NAT (left)
National Screw and Mfg. Company, fastener products. Metal and wood statuette, c. 1960s, 5". $400.00.

Mohawk Tommy (right)
Mohawk Carpet Mills, carpet manufacturing. Ceramic statuette, c. 1960s, 6". $375.00.

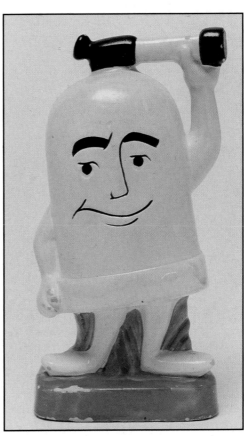

Otto The Orkin Man (left)
Orkin Exterminating Company, Inc., termite and pest control. Metal statuette, c. 1960s, 4". $85.00.

Otto The Orkin Man (right)
Orkin Exterminating Company, Inc., termite and pest control. Papier maché bank, c. 1960s, 8". $900.00.

Raid Bug
S.C. Johnson and Son, Inc., Raid insecticides. Plastic wind-up toy, c. 1980s, 4". $75.00.

Raid Bug
S.C. Johnson and Son, Inc., Raid insecticides. Plastic telephone, c. 1980s, 9". $65.00.

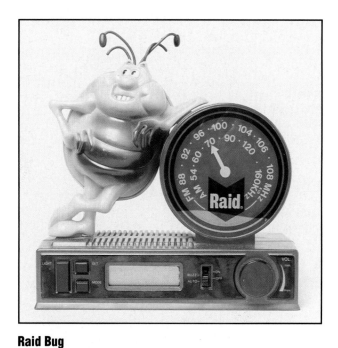

Raid Bug
S.C. Johnson and Son, Inc., Raid insecticides. Plastic clock radio, c. 1980s, 7". $125.00.

Raid Bug
S.C. Johnson and Son, Inc., Raid insecticides. Plastic remote control robot, c. 1980s, 12". $275.00.

Scrubbing Bubble
Dow Chemical Company, disinfectant bathroom cleaner. Molded vinyl squeeze toy, 1989, 3½". $5.00.

Snappy Service (right)
Copper and Brass Sales, Inc., metal supplies. Ceramic bank, c. 1970s, 6". $40.00.

Williams Repairman
J.H. Williams & Company, tools and hardware. Plastic and metal statuette, c. 1980s, 4". $15.00.

World's Strongest Padlock
Master Lock Company, Master padlocks. Painted plaster ashtray, c. 1950s, 7½". $475.00.

Other Drug and Cosmetic Items

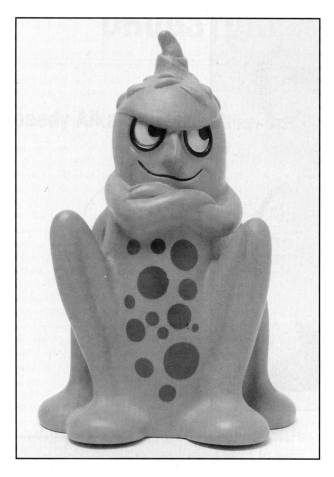

24 Hour Bug
Procter & Gamble, Pepto-Bismol. Molded vinyl bank, c. 1970s, 7". $60.00.

Actigall Gall Bladder
CIBA-GEIGY Corporation, Actigall (ursodiol capsules), medication for gallstones. Molded vinyl squeeze toy, 1989, 7". $30.00.

"A little dab'll do ya"
Beecham Products, Brylcreem hair products. Left: Papier maché bobbin' head, c. 1960s, 5½". $150.00. Above: Two bobbin' heads, c. 1960s, 5½". $275.00 set.

1966 Avon Lady (left)
Avon, perfume and toiletries. Ceramic bottle, 1983, 8". $55.00.

Barking Cough Dog (right)
Bristol Laboratories, Naldecon-CX cough syrup. Composition statuette, c. 1970s, 5". $50.00.

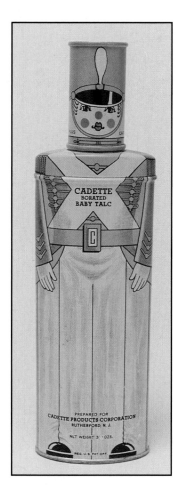

Diaparene Baby (above)
Sterling Drug, Inc., Diaparene baby products. Molded vinyl doll, 1980, 5". $30.00.

SMA Baby (above)
Wyeth Laboratories, SMA and nursery products. Vinyl finger puppet, 1986, 4". $35.00.

Cadette (left)
Cadette Products Corporation, Cadette borated baby talc. Metal container, c. 1950s, 7½". $85.00.

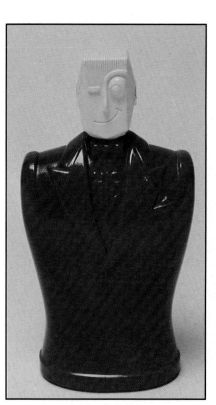

HIS Man (left)
The House For Men, Inc., HIS talc and cologne. Plastic cap and glass bottle, c. 1960s, 6". $75.00.

Mr. Bubble (right)
Gold Seal Company, Mr. Bubble bubble bath. Plastic figural container banks, c. 1970s. 9½" - $95.00; 7" - $80.00.

Mr. Bubble
Airwick Industries, Mr. Bubble bubble bath. Molded vinyl squeeze toy, 1990, 8". $35.00.

Mycitracin Bumpkin
The Upjohn Company, Mycitracin triple antibiotic ointment. Ceramic statuette, 1984, 3½". $30.00.

Taped Crusader
Curity/The Kendall Company, Curad adhesive bandages. Molded vinyl bank, 1977, 7½". $45.00.

Miss Curity (left)
Curity/The Kendall Company, medical bandages and supplies. Plastic store display, c. 1950s, 19". $115.00.

Mr. Ice (right)
Perfume. Plastic store display, c. 1970s, 20". $125.00.

Ritalin Man (above)
CIBA/GEIGY Corporation, Ritalin (methylphenidate), medication for hyperactive child syndrome and depression. Plastic statuette and pen stand, c. 1970s, 7". $70.00.

Ritalin Man (left and right)
CIBA/GEIGY Corporation, Ritalin (methylphenidate), medication for hyperactive child syndrome and depression. Plastic statuette (front and back), c. 1970s, 5½". $200.00.

Sparkle
Procter & Gamble, Crest toothpaste. Plastic telephone, c. 1980s, 11". $30.00.

Tagamet Tommy
Smith Kline & French Laboratories, Tagamet cimetidine capsules, medication for ulcers. PVC statuette, 1988, 5". $17.50.

Tubby
Watkins Products, Inc., Tubby Fun Bath. Plastic figural container, c. 1970s, 5". $35.00.

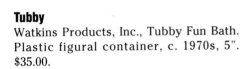

Chapter 12

CLOTHES AND SHOES

Buster Brown Brown Shoe Company

In the May 4, 1902 edition of the *New York Herald*, a new era in newspaper humor began with the first Buster Brown comic strip, "Buster's Bad Bargain." With the birth of the mischievous Buster and his talking dog, Tige, their creator, Richard F. Outcault, became one of the founding fathers of American comics.

The Buster Brown story was that of a prim and properly dressed boy from the average American family – a boy whose behavior was anything but proper. Each strip concluded with Buster's "resolution" to change his ways. In spite of Buster's naughtiness and childish pranks, he became an overnight success.

Outcault used his own children and their dog (Tige is short for Tiger) as models for the comic. Buster's mother was patterned after Mrs. Outcault, and her stylish clothes reflected the latest fashions for ladies. Buster's outfits also had a great impact on children's wear of the time. Although his Lord Fauntleroy clothing was not new to wealthy families, the popularity of the cartoon increased sales of that style of clothing to the new, rapidly growing middle class.

In 1903, the Brown Shoe Company of St. Louis, named after George W. Brown, recognizing the potential value of the Buster Brown name as a juvenile shoe trademark, approached Outcault. Buoyed by his initial success, Outcault established his own advertising agency a year later. At the St. Louis World's Fair, he offered the Buster Brown trademark to more than 40 manufacturers of children's clothing, toys,

china, food, and even cigars and whiskey. One of these manufacturers was the Old Stone Fort Hosiery Mill, subsequently renamed Buster Brown Hosiery, and later Buster Brown Apparel when it expanded to include children's clothing.

Of the more than 100 companies which eventually used the Buster Brown trademark, only the Brown Shoe Company and Buster Brown Apparel have survived. With the jingle, *I'm Buster Brown, I live in a shoe. That's my dog Tige, Look for him there too!*, the Brown Shoe Company promoted its Buster Brown Shoes in advertisements, billboards, radio, and TV. Because of the great number of manufacturers who have used the Buster and Tige trademark, a host of Buster Brown collectibles have kept his legend alive long after Outcault retired the cartoon in the 1920s.

Other Apparel Products

Busters (right)
Brown Group, Inc., Buster's children's shoes. Molded vinyl bank, 1989, 8½". $45.00.

General Jeans (left)
Millers Outpost, clothing store chain. Molded vinyl bank, 1979, 8½". $35.00.

Happy Foot
McGregor, athletic wear and sporting goods. Composition store display, c. 1950s, 16". $500.00.

Hush Puppies
Wolverine Shoe Company, Hush Puppies brand shoes. Molded vinyl bank, c. 1970s, 8". $25.00.

Hush Puppies
Wolverine Shoe Company, Hush Puppies brand shoes. Painted wooden store display, c. 1970s, 8½". $45.00.

King Kaufenberg
Kaufenberg Enterprises, T-shirt manufacturing. Ceramic bank, 1983, 5". $35.00.

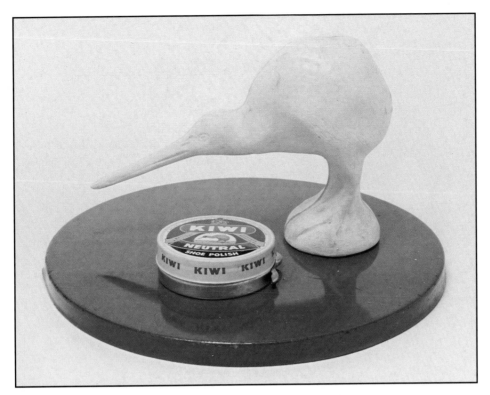

Kiwi
Kiwi Polish Company Ltd., shoe and boot polish. Composition store display, c. 1950s, 4". $35.00.

Lurchi
Salamander (Germany), children's shoes. Vinyl squeeze toy, c. 1980s, 4½". $35.00. Vinyl bendable figure, c. 1980s, 4½". $20.00.

Meltonian Man
Reckitt & Colman, Meltonian polish and shoe creams. Composition store display, c. 1940s, 8½". $300.00.

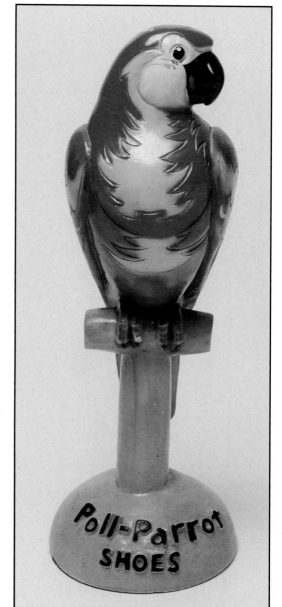

Poll Parrot
Poll Parrot Shoes, shoes. Painted plaster store display, c. 1950s, 15". $250.00.

Red Goose
Red Goose Shoes, shoes and footwear. Plaster statuette, c. 1940s, 5". $30.00.

Weatherbird
Weatherbird Shoes, shoes and footwear. Papier maché bobbin' head, c. 1960s, 7½". $325.00.

Red Goose
Red Goose Shoes, shoes and footwear. Plastic bank, c. 1960s, 5". $15.00.

Seiko Robot
Seiko watches. Plastic and metal store display, c. 1970s, 9". $400.00.

Chapter 13
SERVICE AND UTILITIES

Mr. ZIP   United States Postal Service

The saga of Mr. ZIP recounts the story of one of the most successful trademark identification campaigns in the history of American advertising. In 1963, the U.S. Postal Service proposed to introduce a new, address-zoning number, the ZIP (Zoning Improvement Plan) code. At that time, in addition to rising labor costs, the volume of mail had increased so much that it was getting difficult for the mail to be sorted by hand and still be delivered in a timely fashion. With the advent of computers which could read and sort the mail automatically, the ZIP Code looked like it had real potential to solve the Postal Service's problems.

The idea for Mr. ZIP began on an airplane, when the Postmaster General J. Edward Day chanced to sit beside AT & T's chairman, Frederick Kappel. Upon learning of the Postal Service's preparations to launch the new address-zoning program, Kappell cautioned Day, that unless properly handled, such a course could create a public furor. He suggested that the Postal Service could benefit from the experience AT & T had gained when it introduced all-digital

dialing and area codes. Shortly thereafter, AT & T officials offered the Postal Service a scrawny cartoon character it had named Mr. P.O. Zone as an item which could be used in promoting the new, five-digit code. During a subsequent meeting, "ZIP Code" was adopted as the name for the new system and Mr. P.O. Zone's name was changed to Mr. ZIP.

Mr. ZIP's career, however, did not begin with either AT & T or the Postal Service. He was originally drawn by the artist Howard Wilcox of the ad agency Cunningham and Walsh in the late 1950s. Coincidentally, Wilcox's father was a retired postman. At the time, Chase Manhattan Bank of New York was running a light-hearted campaign to promote its bank-by-mail service. The original, naive and childlike postman was accompanied by the jingle, *"In Rain or Hail, Bank by Mail."* By the time Mr. ZIP reached the Postal Service, he was given a mailbag and sharpened into a dashing figure in blue.

The Mr. ZIP campaign made ZIP Codes a household term and won overwhelming public support. He appeared in newspapers, television, and billboards, extolling the merits of the ZIP Code. The media blitz included Ethel Merman belting out, *"Zip-a-dee-doo-dah, zip-a-dee-ay! Send your mail out the five-digit way!"*

Mr. ZIP's best deliveries came on the sides of mailboxes and selvages of stamps. At the beginning of the campaign, some post offices rigged mailboxes so that when a letter was deposited, Mr. ZIP's voice inquired, *"Thank you. Did you include the ZIP Code?"* Mr. ZIP's illustrious career in public service ended in 1980 with the Postal Service's adoption of the new, ZIP + 4 system. Although in retirement, Mr. ZIP is still a favorite of stamp collectors, some of whom have formed Zippy collector clubs.

Mr. ZIP
U.S. Postal Service, ZIP Code promotions. Wooden pop-up statuette, c. 1960s, 6½". $200.00.

Mr. ZIP
U.S. Postal Service, ZIP Code promotions. Plastic pull toy, c. 1970s, 7½". $145.00.

Reddy Kilowatt Reddy Communications, Inc.

part in the wartime effort, selling war bonds and urging customer cooperation in energy conservation programs. As utilities began using nuclear energy, Reddy starred in the film, *The Mighty Atom.* Reddy also appeared in a host of advertising premiums including jewelry, hand lotion, and statuettes.

Reddy Kilowatt Service is now called Reddy Communications, Inc. The company still provides consulting and communication services to many investor-owned utility companies in the United States and several foreign countries. Reddy Kilowatt, their registered trademark and service mark, is still on active duty, promoting goodwill and wise energy use.

"Reddy Kilowatt" is a registered trademark and is used here with permission of Reddy Communications, Inc., Albuquerque, New Mexico.

Reddy Kilowatt was the creation of Ashton B. Collins, a merchandising manager with the Alabama Power Company. On a stormy afternoon in 1926, Collins watched flashes of lightning form the image of a figure against the darkened sky. With this inspiration, Collins sketched the first Reddy. He later added a smiling face, a light bulb nose, receptacle ears, and rubber safety boots and named him "Reddy Kilowatt, Your Electrical Servant."

Over the next seven years, Collins held a variety of positions within the electrical industry. He showed a natural talent as a speaker and promotional innovator. All the while, he was refining the Reddy Kilowatt concept. In 1934, he formed his own company, Reddy Kilowatt Service, offering public relations and marketing services to electric utility companies. Included in his marketing program was his licensed trademark star, Reddy Kilowatt. Philadelphia Electric was the first company to sign on, with Reddy making his print debut in 1934. Before long, more than two hundred companies were part of the Reddy Kilowatt Program.

In an industry that could easily come across as impersonal, Reddy offered a warm, humanizing influence. He appeared on electrical company signs, promotions, and advertising. Utility bills were easier to pay with the friendly Reddy saying, *"Howdy, folks, here's my bill for the work I've done."* Reddy did his

Reddy Kilowatt
Reddy Kilowatt, Inc., electrical company promotions. Wooden statue, c. 1950s, 12". $375.00.

Reddy Kilowatt (left)
Reddy Kilowatt, Inc., electrical company promotions. Plastic glow-in-the-dark statuette, 1961, 6". $125.00.

Reddy Kilowatt (right)
Reddy Kilowatt, Inc., electrical company promotions. Papier maché bobbin' head, c. 1960s, 6½". $575.00.

Reddy Kilowatt
Reddy Kilowatt, Inc., electrical company promotions. Plastic statuettes, c. 1950s, 6". $150.00 each.

Smokey Bear   U.S. Department of Agriculture, Forest Service

Smokey Bear was created in 1944 for an advertising campaign to help prevent forest fires. The first drawing of Smokey was contracted and done by Albert Staehle. In 1946, Rudy Wendelin took over as the U.S. Department of Agriculture's artist. For many years, Wendelin painted the image of Smokey Bear with his ranger hat, blue jeans, and shovel. "Remember... Only *You* Can Prevent Forest Fires!" became Smokey's slogan in 1947. He was granted special trademark status by an act of Congress (PL 82-359).

In 1950, a black bear cub which had been orphaned and injured by a fire was found in the Lincoln National Forest of New Mexico. The cub was named Smokey and became the real-life counterpart to the poster bear. His story has been recounted in a comic book issued by the Forest Service since 1960. He lived at the National Zoo in Washington, DC until 1976. Smokey Bear turned 50 years old August 9, 1994!

Smokey Bear
U.S. Department of Agriculture, Forest Service, forest fire prevention. Plastic bank, c. 1970s, 8". $40.00.

Smokey Bear
U.S. Department of Agriculture, Forest Service, forest fire prevention. Ceramic salt and pepper shakers, c. 1960s, 4". $35.00 set.

Other Service or Utility Related Products

Captain Marine
Marine Bank, financial services. Molded vinyl bank, c. 1980s, 8½". $35.00.

insty-prints Wizard
insty-prints, Inc., commercial printing services. Molded vinyl bank, c. 1980s, 9". $115.00.

Handy Flame
Gas utility company promotion. Ceramic salt and pepper shakers, c. 1950s, 4". $25.00.

AMÖ
Allimpex internationale spedition gmbH, international delivery services. Plastic pull toy, c. 1970s, 5". $30.00.

Saguaro Cactus
Saguaro Savings and Loan Association, financial services. Plastic bank, c. 1980s, 6½". $35.00.

Save at Watkins
Watkins Department Stores. Ceramic bank, c. 1950s, 5½". $75.00.

Shawmut Indian
Shawmut Bank (Boston, MA), financial services. Sebastian miniature, 1986, 4". $50.00.

Mutual of Omaha
Mutual of Omaha Companies, insurance and financial services. Plastic bank, c. 1980s, 4½". $65.00.

The Big One
Security Homestead, financial services. Ceramic bank, c. 1970s, 7". $75.00.

"We Hop To It"
Burlington Northern, air and train freight. Plastic wind-up toy, c. 1980s, 4½". $40.00.

Willie Wiredhand
National Rural Electric Cooperative, electric utility company promotions. Rubber and plastic statuette, c. 1960s, 10½". $750.00.

Willie Wiredhand
Kay Electric Cooperative, electric utility company promotions. Metal statuette, 1975, 4". $300.00.

Woodsy Owl
U.S. Department of Agriculture, Forest Service, anti-litter promotions. Ceramic bank, c. 1970s, 8½". $75.00.

Chapter 14

TRAVEL AND ENTERTAINMENT

Alfred E. Neuman *Mad* Magazine

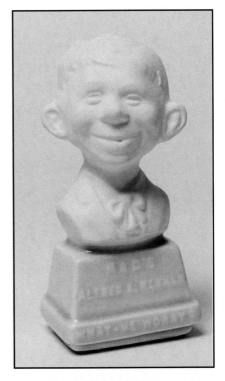

Although Alfred E. Neuman is best known as *Mad* Magazine's "cover guy," he actually has been around since the turn of the century. His idiotic, grinning freckled-face, accompanied by the words "What, Me Worry?" was originally a folk creation, appearing on postcards and small-business advertisements. In fact, it was on such a postcard, tacked to a friend's bulletin board, that a *Mad* editor first saw the goofy-looking kid. He named him after Alfred Newman, a composer-conductor on the Henry Morgan radio show. Somehow the added middle initial gave Alfred E. Neuman just the right ring of insignificance. After appearing in a *Mad* paperback book, "the face" appeared on a *Mad* magazine cover as a 1956 write-in candidate for President. The balloting didn't go so well but *Mad* had found its new trademark spokesman.

Alfred E. Neuman (top photo)
E.C. Publications, *Mad* Magazine. Ceramic statuette, c. 1960s, 4½". $250.00.

Alfred E. Neuman (bottom photo)
E.C. Publications, *Mad* Magazine. Rubber bendable figure, 1988, 8". $20.00.

Kraft TV Theatre Cameraman   Kraft Inc.

Kraft TV Theatre Cameraman!

The Kraft Television Theatre was one of the country's most popular TV programs in the 1950s. Known for its gripping, live theatrical dramas, the show appeared every Wednesday and Thursday night. Before each episode, a lilliputian Kraft TV cameraman rolled across the screen, with camera swiveling. So many viewers wrote Kraft to ask if they could get a souvenir of the little guy that Kraft finally issued a replica premium in 1954. Fifty cents and the end flap of a Velveeta carton and he was yours!

Kraft TV Theatre Cameraman
Kraft, Inc., Kraft Television Theater. Plastic statuette pull toy, 1954, 4½". $110.00.

Sleepy Bear   Travelodge

In the early 1950s, Travelodge was still a modest chain of motels and lodges for the weary highway traveler. The company, looking for a promotional mascot, decided upon a bear. At that time, Travelodge was strictly a California chain; therefore, a bear trademark would coincide with the state's emblem – the California Golden Bear.

As Travelodge was in the business of selling sleep, the company decided to call the bear, "Sleepy," a big departure from his ferocious, state flag counterpart. The first company logo began as a sleepy-eyed, furry bear with one paw and leg extended – sleepwalking. The bear was eventually given a long-sleeved nightshirt and a white nightcap which bore his name.

Sleepy became so popular that the company developed the successful slogan –*"Sleepy Bear is Everywhere."* And he was! His somnambulistic image appeared on a wide variety of items at each motel. In fact, parents could even buy a soft, fuzzy Sleepy teddy bear for their children to cuddle up with at night.

In 1971, the Sleepy Bear logo was modernized into a simple, orange silhouette of the sleepwalking bear. In addition to its use on company signs, stationery, and flags, the sleepy image can be found on a host of items sold at each motel's gift shop. Travelodge was honored in 1972 by the James B. Beam Distilling Company when Sleepy was cast as the image for a bourbon whiskey bottle. Those who can't get enough of Sleepy might consider joining the "Sleepy Bear Club" when staying at a Travelodge.

Sleepy Bear
Travelodge, motel chain. Jim Beam Bourbon whiskey bottle (both sides shown), 1972, 12". $40.00.

Sleepy Bear
Travelodge, motel chain. Molded vinyl squeeze toy, c. 1970s, 5½". $35.00.

Miscellaneous Products

Berti
W. Goebel Porzellanfabrik, Goebel collectibles. Molded vinyl squeeze toy, c. 1970s, 2½". $15.00.

Big Aggie
WNAX, radio station promotion. Plaster bank, c. 1940s, 8". $250.00.

Bully
Bully GMBH (West Germany), toys and PVC figurines. PVC figurine, c. 1980s, 1". $10.00.

Chico (left)
Santa Fe Railway, railroad transportation. Composition statuette, c. 1970s, 7". $250.00.

Esky – "You Saw It In *Esquire*" (right)
Esquire Magazine. Composition store display, c. 1950s, 9". $500.00.

Esky
Esquire Magazine. Composition store display, c. 1940s, 25". $650.00.

Esky
Esquire Magazine. Composition store display, c. 1940s, 11". $665.00.

Indian on Flying Carpet
Air India, airline and travel services. Composition store displays, c. 1970s. 12" – $65.00; 17" – $75.00.

Indian on Flying Carpet
Air India, airline and travel services. Painted plaster statuette, c. 1970s, 4½". $17.50.

Mackinac Mac
Detroit and Mackinac Railroad, railroad transportation. Composition statuette, c. 1940s, 7". $350.00.

Magic Marxie
Louis Marx and Company, toys. Plastic in-house figurine, c. 1960s, 1". $50.00.

Mario (left)
Nintendo of America, Inc., Super Mario Bros and Nintendo Entertainment systems. Plastic water squirter, 1988, 6". $15.00.
Geoffrey (center)
Toys R Us, Inc., toy store chain. Plastic flashlight, 1989, 8½". $20.00.
Rich Uncle Pennybags (right)
Parker Bros., Monopoly. Ceramic bank, c. 1980s, 6½". $35.00.

Mascotte Ufficiale
Col Italia '90, Italia '90 World Cup. Plastic statuette, 1990, 5½". $60.00.

The Menehune of Hawaii
United Airlines, airline and travel services. Molded vinyl bank, c. 1970s, 9½". $75.00.

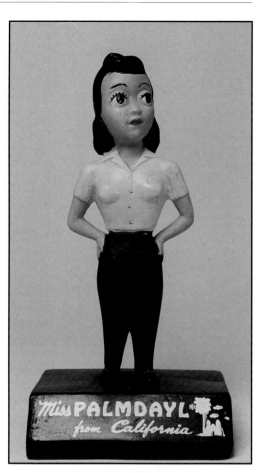

The Menehune of Hawaii (left)
United Airlines, airline and travel services. Composition store display, c. 1970s, 22". $75.00.

Miss Palmdayl (right)
California industry promotion. Composition statuette, c. 1940s, 9". $275.00.

Nugget Sam (left)
Dick Grave's Nugget (Sparks, NV), hotel and casino. Rubber squeeze toy, c. 1950s, 12". $35.00.

Nugget Sam (right)
Dick Grave's Nugget (Sparks, NV), hotel and casino. Papier maché bobbin' head, c. 1960s, 6½". $185.00.

Nugget Sam
Dick Grave's Nugget (Sparks, NV), hotel and casino. Ceramic salt and pepper shakers, c. 1960s, 4". $30.00 set.

Nugget Sam (left)
Dick Grave's Nugget (Sparks, NV), hotel and casino. Ceramic ashtray, c. 1960s, 3½". $45.00.

Pedro (right)
South of the Border, tourist complex, motel and restaurant. Ceramic figurine, c. 1960s, 5". $30.00.

Pac-Man
Midway Mfg. Company, Pac-Man video games. Molded vinyl squeeze toy, c. 1980s, 2". $10.00.

Penguin (right)
Penguin Books Ltd., publishing. Royal Doulton china statuette, c. 1970s, 5". $150.00.

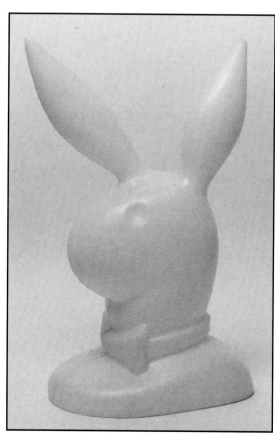

Pin Money Pete (left)
Spare Time, bowling products. Plastic bank, 1984, 6½". $20.00.

Playboy Rabbit (right)
Playboy Enterprises, Inc., magazine and entertainment services. Plastic table display (Playboy Club), c. 1970s, 28". $165.00.

Red Book
RB Books, publishing. Plastic store display, c. 1970s, 9". $300.00.

Stay Puft Marshmallow Man
Columbia Pictures, fictional product in *Ghostbusters* movie. Molded vinyl squeeze toy, 1984, 7". $7.50.

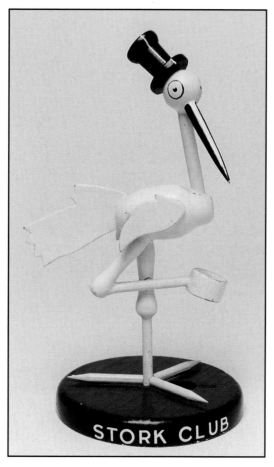

Stork
The Stork Club restaurant. Wooden table display and vase, c. 1950s, 7½". $100.00.

Tex Tan Man
Tex Tan. PVC figurine, c. 1970s, 6". $55.00.

Varig Bird
Varig Airlines (Brazil), airline and travel services. Composition rubber statuette, c. 1970s, 5". $250.00.

Chapter 15

TOBACCO PRODUCTS

Willie the Kool Penguin Brown & Williamson Tobacco Corporation ——————

Willie the Kool Penguin came on the scene in 1933 when Kool cigarettes were introduced. Brown & Williamson decided that the unique menthol taste of Kool cigarettes could best be represented by a penguin. Willie appeared on billboards, print ads, and radio through the 1930s and 1940s. Kool television commercials in the 1950s were filled with promises of smoking delight typical of that period – *"Switch from hots"* with the turban-topped Willie walking on a bed of coals *"to snow fresh Kools,"* with Willie skating on an icy lake, holding a pack of Kool cigarettes.

Willie has been immortalized in a variety of wares – salt and pepper shakers, key chains, cigarette lighters, and even jewelry. It was during modeling for the salt and pepper shakers that Willie met his wife, Millie. He retired from the hectic pace of spokesbird in the late 1950s.

Willie as "Dr. Kool"
Brown & Williamson Tobacco Corporation, Kool cigarettes. Painted plaster statuette, c. 1950s, 4½". $125.00.

Willie and Millie
Brown & Williamson Tobacco Corporation, Kool cigarettes. Plastic salt and pepper shakers, c. 1950s, 3". $15.00.

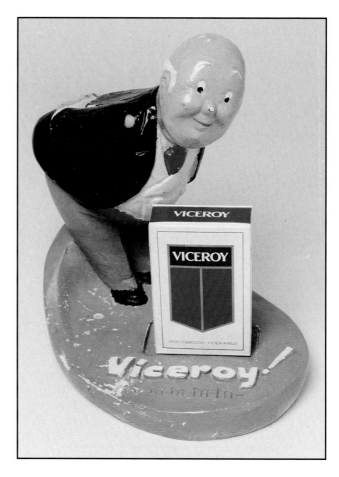

Joe Camel
R.J. Reynolds Tobacco USA, Camel cigarettes. Vinyl can cooler, 1991, 4". $10.00.

Viceroy Butler (right)
Brown & Williamson Tobacco Corporation, Viceroy cigarettes. Plaster store display, c. 1950s, 8". $275.00.

Sir Walter Raleigh
Brown & Williamson Tobacco Corporation, Raleigh cigarettes. Metal statuette, c. 1960s, 5". $35.00.

BIBLIOGRAPHY

"A Great Name in Oil, Sinclair through Fifty Years." Sinclair Oil Corporation, 1966.

"Century of Discovery, An Exxon Album." Exxon Corporation, 1982.

Diamant, Lincoln.
Television's Classic Commercials, The Golden Years 1948–1958. Hastings House, Publishers, 1958.

Goodsell, Dan, "Funny Face Facts Newsletter," 1991.

Harris, Moira.
The Paws of Refreshment, The Story of Hamm's Beer Advertising. Pogo Press, 1990.

Hall, Jim.
Mighty Minutes. Harmony Books, 1984.

Marguette, Arthur.
Brands, Trademarks and Good Will, The Story of The Quaker Oats Company. McGraw-Hill Book Company, 1967.

McGhie, Juliet. "Tale of the Tiger in The Lamp." Exxon Corporation, Summer 1984.

Morgan, Hal
Symbols of America. Penguin Books, 1986.

Morton, Jim.
Pop Void. Pop Void Publications, 1987.

Preziosi, Don. "The Man from MAD." *Postcard Collector,* August 1987.

Robison, Joleen and Sellers, Kay.
Advertising Dolls. Collector Books, 1980.

"Y & R" and "Broadcasting, Radio and Television Advertising." The Museum of Broadcasting, 1988.

INDEX

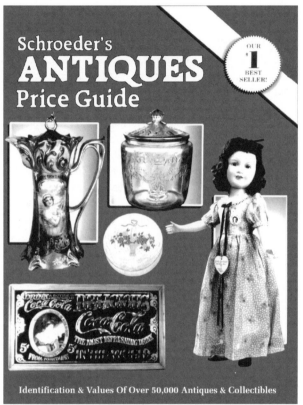